JOYCE WIELAND'S
THE FAR SHORE

The Far Shore (1976), made under the direction of celebrated visual artist and experimental filmmaker Joyce Wieland, is one of Canada's most innovative contributions to cinema. The film borrows elements from the life of Canadian painter Tom Thomson, who is represented by the character of Tom McLeod. The main character, however, is not Tom, but the fictional protagonist Eulalie de Chicoutimi, the married Québécoise woman who falls in love with him. Using Eulalie's perspective, Wieland reframes Thomson's life and story as a romantic melodrama while infusing it with subversive commentary on gender, nature, and nationalism and, ultimately, on the value of art.

Here, Wieland specialist Johanne Sloan offers a fascinating new perspective on *The Far Shore*, making it more accessible by discussing Wieland's utopian fusion of art and politics, the importance of landscape within Canadian culture, and the ongoing struggle over the meaning of the natural environment.

JOHANNE SLOAN is an associate professor in the Department of Art History at Concordia University.

CANADIAN CINEMA 4

JOYCE WIELAND'S

THE FAR SHORE

JOHANNE SLOAN

UNIVERSITY OF TORONTO PRESS
Toronto Buffalo London

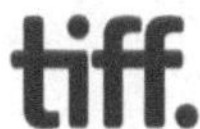

Toronto Buffalo London
utorontopress.com

ISBN: 978-1-4426-4127-3 (cloth)
ISBN: 978-1-4426-1060-6 (paper)

Library and Archives Canada Cataloguing in Publication

Sloan, Johanne
Joyce Wieland's The far shore / Johanne Sloan.

(Canadian cinema ; 4)
Includes bibliographical references.
ISBN: 978-1-4426-4127-3 (bound) ISBN: 978-1-4426-1060-6 (pbk.)

1. Wieland, Joyce, 1930–1998 – Criticism and interpretation.
2. Far shore (Motion picture). I. Title. II. Title: Far shore.
III. Series: Canadian cinema (Toronto, Ont.) ; 4.

PN1997.F3444S56 2010 791.430233092 C2010-902279-X

Cover image: Courtesy of the Canadian Filmmakers Distribution Centre (CFMDC)

TIFF and the University of Toronto Press acknowledge the financial assistance of the Ontario Media Development Corporation, the Canada Council for the Arts, and the Ontario Arts Council.

Canada Council for the Arts Conseil des Arts du Canada

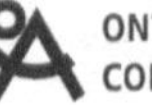
ONTARIO ARTS COUNCIL
CONSEIL DES ARTS DE L'ONTARIO

This book has been published with the help of a grant from the Canadian Federation for the Humanities and Social Sciences, through the Aid to Scholarly Publications Programme, using funds provided by the Social Sciences and Humanities Research Council of Canada.

University of Toronto Press acknowledges the financial support of its publishing activities of the Government of Canada through the Book Publishing Industry Development Program (BPIDP).

Contents

Acknowledgments

I'd like to thank the friends, colleagues, and students who have listened to me rant and enthuse about Joyce Wieland over the years. The staff at the National Gallery of Canada's Library and Archives have been consistently helpful throughout this research project, and I have benefited greatly from their expertise. Judy Steed was extremely open and generous and provided valuable insights into the making of *The Far Shore*, and I am very grateful to her. I'd also like to thank Mark Clintberg for his inestimable skills as a researcher for this project.

JOYCE WIELAND'S

THE FAR SHORE

Introduction

Joyce Wieland's feature-length film *The Far Shore* (1976) tells a story built around the historical personage of Tom Thomson, the Canadian painter who drowned in Canoe Lake in 1917. There is indeed a surrogate Thomson figure in the film, named Tom, and yet he is not the central character: *The Far Shore* introduces an entirely fictional protagonist, a woman from Quebec called Eulalie, who comes to Toronto as the wife of a wealthy engineer/entrepreneur and falls in love with Tom. It is because the film adopts her point of view, because we perceive the artist as the object of her desire, that the usual account of Thomson's art and life is transformed into a more complex and melodramatic narrative. Not only are the biographical details of Thomson's life rearranged through Wieland's film, but so too is his legacy of landscape paintings seen anew. The famous wilderness imagery that is so often used to express a conservative Canadian nationalism acquires a different set of meanings in *The Far Shore*.

In a telling comment Wieland announced that *The Far Shore* would articulate a politicized approach to landscape and nationhood, but as she wanted to avoid a didactic presentation of politics, she was intent on taking that political edge, and 'embedding it into a very romantic script.'[1] Wieland often spoke of herself as a political artist, and it is true that feminist, ecological, countercultural, and socialist ideas are pervasive, if sometimes camouflaged, throughout her artistic and cinematic practice. Somehow, then, a serious political message would be 'embedded' in this melodramatic portrayal of one woman's love life. How can we interpret the significance of this artistic gesture? I want to argue that Wieland's fictional Eulalie character is sent into the past to rescue Tom Thomson, in a manner of speaking. Eulalie's intense love for Tom (the fictional Tom McLeod) calls into question why it is that 'we' love Tom (the real-life Tom Thomson). This 'we' corresponds only to a phantasmatic collectivity, of course – the dream of a homogeneous Canadian population for whom Tom Thomson is the very epitome of national territory and national character alike. This figuration of the artist has long functioned as a closed semantic circuit, where the meanings of art and land and identity merely confirm each other, without the possibility of change. Wieland's film encourages us to ask questions regarding the ritualistic outpouring of national affection for Tom Thomson: What is the appropriate (or inappropriate) way to manifest this love? Should other Canadian artists receive the same degree of public veneration that has been accorded Thomson?[2] Is it possible to actively despise Tom Thomson (and his Group of Seven confederates) and still be a good Canadian?

By the 1970s, when Joyce Wieland came to make her film, this body of landscape art had already become 'blue-chip tokens of wise investment,'[3] and, perhaps more disturbingly, Tom Thomson's artworks had been subjected to a kind of institutional and ideological calcification. Wieland's revisionist film shows that she did not accept this fixity of meaning and, in my reading, *The Far Shore* is an attempt to recuperate a genuinely utopian impulse in the art of Thomson and his friends. The film restages the last months of Thomson's life to show that a vision of landscape emerges as the result of a struggle: the natural environment comes into focus according to imperatives that are simultaneously commercial, geopolitical, and aesthetic, while we are also shown how the characters' personal histories and desires are interwoven with this complex encounter with the land. In *The Far Shore* this register of subjective desire becomes most evident through the figure of Eulalie. It is the imaginative force of her troubled persona and the very excess of her love for Tom which allow the politically conservative Thomson icon to be dislodged, to be replaced by a more open symbol of Canadian cultural identity.

Much scholarship in recent years has sought to demystify Tom Thomson and the Group of Seven painters (insofar as these artists have been made to play a role as consolidators of Canadian identity), and Wieland's project can certainly be understood in these terms, with one vital proviso: alongside this critical impulse, a deliberate re-mythification process is also set in motion by the film. Some of the more insightful and sympathetic reviews of *The Far Shore* at the time of its release did indeed remark on a myth-like or fable-like quality Wieland was able to achieve with this film. One author commented, 'the plot proceeds with the force of some ancient myth.'[4] This does, however, point to one of the more perplexing qualities of *The Far Shore*, that it follows many naturalistic cinematic conventions, even while some of the most powerful imagery in the film boasts a mythic (non-naturalistic) dimension. Wieland's film thus does not deliver up the definitive, 'real' Tom Thomson, but rather ensures that the figure of Thomson remains a cipher, an ever elusive object of (Canadian) desire.

Description of the Plot

The Far Shore tells the story of Eulalie de Chicoutimi, a cultured woman from rural Quebec, who comes to Toronto in 1919 as the bride of Ross Turner, a successful engineer and entrepreneur who also has political ambitions. Unhappy in her marriage and thwarted in her ambition to become a concert pianist, Eulalie becomes close to the painter Tom McLeod, a fictional character based on the historical figure of Tom

Thomson. (As there is a great deal of overlap between the painter-character created by Wieland and his historical counterpart, I have chosen to refer to the fictional character in the film as 'Tom,' while using the designations 'Tom Thomson' or 'Thomson' to refer to the actual person who died in 1917.) The film shows that Tom and Ross had been friendly but fall out when Tom refuses to guide an exploration party looking for silver on Ross's land. On this occasion Ross's sidekick Cluny (his onetime army superior when both fought in the First World War) starts a fight, which ends with Tom physically throwing Cluny out of his house – the shack he inhabits in the quasi-rural terrain of a Toronto ravine. Ross's behaviour becomes increasingly unpleasant; the insensitivity he showed in early scenes is replaced by outright aggression. In a disturbing scene, he enters the couple's bedroom and brutally forces himself on Eulalie. Meanwhile, Eulalie and Tom become close and appear to fall in love, as she repeatedly visits him in his shack, in scenes of intimacy and pleasurable domesticity. Ultimately, though, spring arrives and Tom leaves the city without declaring himself. In harsh parting words Eulalie accuses him of being 'in love with a rock and a tree and a piece of sky.' Eulalie then falls into a depressed state, while her husband imagines that she still pines for an old fiancé.

Over an hour into the film, the action relocates to the 'north country,' which the viewer now understands to be the site of competing interests – commercial, political, artistic, libidinal. All of the main characters are there: Eulalie, Tom, Ross, and Cluny. Tom is painting and camping on one side of the lake, while on another side is a well-appointed lodge where a picnic is under way, even as some preliminary searching for silver is going on nearby. In this natural environment, actions and reactions accelerate quickly: an explosion injures another member of the party, and Eulalie and Tom catch sight of each other across a stretch of water. Commanded by her husband to return to the house and then to the city, Eulalie refuses, and then, hearing that Ross and Cluny intend to harass or harm Tom, she disables the available watercraft, smashing the canoe with an axe and throwing the rowboat's oars into the water. When Ross comes towards her, she knocks him down with a paddle. Having assaulted her husband and destroyed his property, Eulalie dives into the lake fully clothed and swims across a wide expanse of water to Tom's canoe (fig. I.1). The remaining minutes of the film consist of the lovers' being pursued by Ross and Cluny, the two canoes criss-crossing the starkly beautiful scenery. There is an interlude of lovemaking, in which both Eulalie and Tom are immersed in the lake, but even this scene cannot escape the sense of doom and persecution that now dominates the film. Shortly after arguing with Cluny about their inability to locate Eulalie and Tom because they cannot 'get the lay of the land,' Ross notices the lovers drift silently by. He seems to be in shock and does not respond, but shots ring out as Cluny shoots them with his rifle. We see the body of Tom jerk forward. We see the overturned canoe, a bloody bullet-hole in Tom's back, and Eulalie's hat floating on the water. The camera lingers on the surface of the water for some moments, and then the film is over.

The Critical Reception

Joyce Wieland was a well-known artist and experimental filmmaker when she set out to make *The Far Shore* as a full-length feature film. The idea for the film was first publicly proposed when she introduced fragments of a script in a bookwork, as part of her 1971 solo exhibition at the National Gallery of Canada. The film was announced as 'True Patriot Love: A Canadian Love, Technology, Leadership and Art Story ... A movie by Joyce Wieland.' During 1973 and 1974 Wieland joined forces with Judy Steed, herself a filmmaker and a social activist in sympathy with Wieland's project, who came on board to help to raise money for the film. After an extended period of negotiation, the Canadian Film

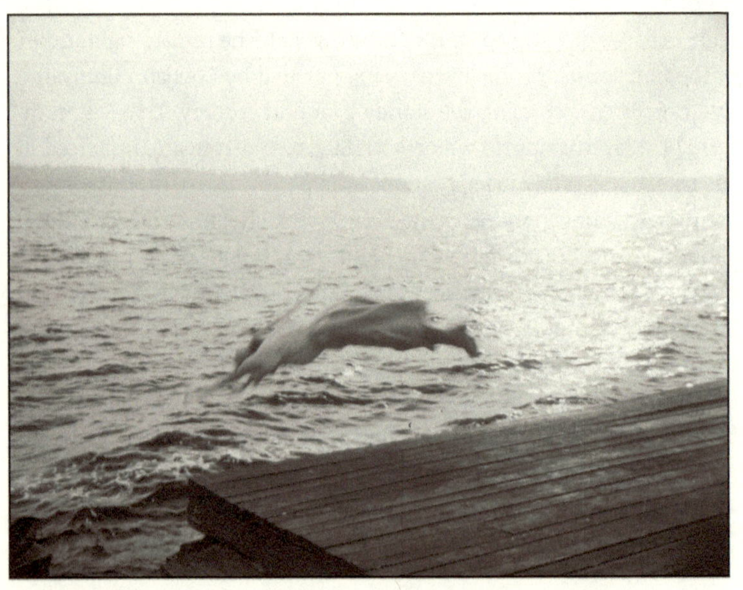

I.1. Eulalie dives fully clothed into the lake. National Gallery of Canada, Library and Archives, Ottawa.

Development Corporation (CFDC) agreed to contribute $200,000 towards the film, to match an amount Wieland was supposed to raise from other sources. Eventually, with contributions from Famous Players and a number of private donors, the budget went up to $450,000, and Pierre Lamy (the producer known for his work on many important French-language Quebec films of the 1970s) signed on as executive producer and Steed received credit as associate producer. Wieland had been working on the script for a long time and had begun to produce a sequence of elaborate storyboards as well when she contacted Brian Barney to further develop the script, and he then became responsible for the final screenplay. Wieland worked closely with the cinematographer Richard Leiterman and the production designer Anne Pritchard throughout the making of the film.

The casting was not easily accomplished, as there was some pressure from the CFDC to find a well-known male lead to play the role of Tom; Stacey Keach and Donald Sutherland were two of the actors considered, and it is amusing to consider what Sutherland might have done with the role.[5] In the end, it was the lesser-known actor Frank Moore who played Tom and, after much searching, the Québécoise Céline Lomez (fresh from acting in two Denys Arcand films) who took on the role of Eulalie. Moore might not bear much physical resemblance to Tom Thomson (although the surviving photographs of the artist are somehow not very revealing), as his colouring is lighter and his features more delicate, but the actor projected a quiet intensity and dignity that seem appropriate for the famous artist. The vivacious dark-haired Lomez convincingly projects a sense of pent-up longing and emotional fervour even when her spoken lines are few. The Toronto-based actors Lawrence Benedict and Sean McCann played the parts of Ross and Cluny, respectively; a few other characters are seen in passing, but the film is quite closely focused on the interactions between these four. Filming was completed in 1975. A Rosedale mansion was used for the Toronto scenes, while Bon Echo Park in southeastern Ontario provided the setting for the 'north country' scenes, standing in for Algonquin Park, the place Tom Thomson returned to repeatedly in the final years of his life. In addition, the film crew meticulously constructed a replica of the simple shack, inhabited by Thomson during the winters of 1916 and 1917.

The Far Shore premiered in Toronto in 1976, and from the time of its release the response to this film has been remarkably varied, ranging from hyperbolic praise to sharp criticism, in both the popular press and more specialized film publications. In *Chatelaine*, Michele Landsberg wrote that '*The Far Shore* is perhaps the most lushly beautiful movie ever made' and a 'splendid evening's entertainment,'[6] while Lisl Levinsohn complained in *Maclean's* of the film's 'utterly conventional stereotypes,' and its 'bouncing ball of bathos.'[7] In the pages of *Cinema Canada*, soon after the film's release, Barbara Halpern Martineau wrote an extensive review, which admiringly described its style and narrative structure,[8] while the same journal published Douglas Ord's hostile review essay a year later. Ord admitted that he was 'angry that Joyce Wieland had taken someone like Tom Thomson, and made him a sponge for all of her fantasies about Art, and for all of her neuroses about men.'[9] He also went on to blame her and her kind (feminists? overly politicized artists?) for the lamentable state of Canadian cinema.

If *The Far Shore* seemed to elicit strong reactions, this was not the first time Joyce Wieland had had to contend with a vociferous and divided public response to her artistic interventions. At the time of the 1971 National Gallery exhibition mentioned above, Wieland was accused of being either too nationalistic or too cavalier with nationalist symbols. Some commentators hailed the inventiveness of her play with materiality and iconography, whereas others declared the results of this playfulness to be too anti-American, or too 'housewifey' (because of the embroidery, needlework, and cushion-like objects),[10] or simply too prone to comedy. Indeed, Wieland would say about those negative responses to the exhibition: 'they didn't like my sense of humor in relation to nationalist politics.'[11] So it is rather ironic that only a few years later it was not a sense of humour, but rather the sense of tragedy, myth, and melodrama that Wieland brought to the question of nationalism (and to the representation of a national icon like Thomson) that some commentators obviously found too much to take. It could be said, though, that Wieland's unevenly received foray into melodrama put her in good company; Claude Jutra's *Kamouraska* from 1973, for instance, was judged to be a failure by some critics, including Vincent Canby in the *New York Times*, who described it as a failed experiment with the melodrama genre. And if melodramas were particularly undervalued at this time, there are not many commercially released Canadian films from this period that found both critical acclaim and box office success.

As mentioned above, the myth-like or fable-like quality of the film struck several reviewers, although this characteristic could be construed either positively or negatively. In the pages of *Séquences*, André Leroux berated Wieland for her attempt to revivify the mythic dimension of Tom Thomson for nationalistic purposes: 'une oeuvre qui déforme la réalité au profit de la fiction et qui ne fait que mythifier la vie déjà assez mythique de Tom Thomson' (a work that distorts reality for the sake of fiction but that serves only to further mythify the sufficiently mythified life of Tom Thomson). He goes on to assert: 'L'œuvre picturale de Thomson est trop connue pour être ainsi utilisée dans un cadre fictif' (The pictorial work of Thomson is too well known to be used in such a fictional context).[12] Another author who challenged Wieland's ability to master this mythic dimension was Katherine Gilday, writing in the journal *Books in Canada*: 'Wieland proves incapable of coming to creative terms with the very imaginative comprehension of the northern landscape that she has undertaken to apotheosize into myth.'[13] On the positive side, Martineau likened the entire structure and style of the film to fable: 'It is a fable expressed in the form of a melodrama, shot in a clear, carefully framed yet flowing style, edited according to a structure of large segments composed of scenes linked by dissolves, beginning with a frame filled with sky and clouds, ending with a frame filled by dark water.'[14] Peter Harcourt also contended that Wieland's decisions about character and narrative were 'right for the film in terms of fable.' He suggested that if 'psychological realism and narrative action are the essential stuff of the movies ... in *The Far Shore,* Joyce Wieland inverts these expectations. The characters are less important as characters than for what they represent.'[15]

The question of how Wieland approached the representation of the natural world would elicit equally contradictory responses. Paul Gardner, writing for the American publication *Variety*, gave the film a very favourable review overall, suggesting it could become an art-house hit, and he singled out Leiterman's cinematographic rendering of natural scenery as one of *The Far Shore*'s most appealing features.[16] Several other authors wrote admiringly of this aspect of the film. The above-mentioned Gilday is a dissenting voice in this respect, for she writes with evident frustration (and at some length) about how the film fails to do justice to the natural, exterior locations. After the comment about Wieland's unsuccessful attempt to transform the landscape into myth, the critique continues: 'Instead of using the medium's elastic capacities for suggesting altered states of consciousness to probe Tom's relationship with the land, the film-maker grasps the first opportunity to thrust us back into the constraints of interior space.'[17]

Gilday's comments are worth singling out, because this book does focus on the aesthetics of landscape, and this particular author is both eloquent and perceptive in her criticism. Gilday evidently expected that *The Far Shore* would 'probe Tom's relationship to the land,' which is to say, the film would provide insights into a painter's imaginative processes. Wieland eventually does show the artist engaged in *plein-air* activity and we also see the screen filled with expanses of forest and lake, but according to this critic, something is still missing from the picture, as overall the film fails to deliver an aesthetically satisfying landscape experience. To some extent I agree with this assessment: *The Far Shore* does not reveal the landscape painter entirely alone and immersed in nature or caught up in an expressive frenzy as he paints the landscape around him, nor does the film attempt to mimic the distinctively Group-of-Seven composition or coloration.[18] Moreover, by the time the 'north country' (the Bon Echo Park location) is made visually available to the viewer, the narrative has developed in such a way that we are impeded from merely enjoying the scenery: the landscape space as rendered cinematically by Wieland is now the very space within which the lovers are being hunted down; this potentially gorgeous natural environment will shortly become a killing ground. So it is true that Wieland denies the viewer an easily pleasurable visual access to the landscape. This brings us to the latter part of Gilday's critical comment, that the film seems to relentlessly 'thrust us back into the constraints of interior space.' What Gilday construes as the film's flaws, however, can be understood as its most innovative aesthetic qualities. The dialectical tension between the exteriority of landscape and the 'constraints of interior space' points to the film's greatest strength – its complex visual articulation of the natural environment.

Although *The Far Shore* would eventually be hailed by feminist film scholars, the distribution of positive and negative responses to the film at the time of its release cannot be neatly categorized along gender lines, as some women hated it and some men showered it with praise. It was indeed several years after the film's release that feminist scholars came along to explore and theorize the 'constraints of interior space' as an integral aspect of Wieland's *The Far Shore*. In the 1980s one of the most sustained and valuable intellectual responses to *The Far Shore* came from Lauren Rabinovitz, whose scholarship helped to establish Wieland's work as a notable contribution to feminist art, cinema, and theory. Through critical texts and interviews, Rabinovitz has suggested that Wieland's 'attempt to create a commercially viable feminist cinema' involved a re-appropriation of the melodrama genre.[19] The homage to melodrama had been noticed by some earlier authors, such as Martineau, but more specific links to the melodramatic 'women's picture' within film history had not been unravelled. Rabinovitz (perhaps as an American) is much less preoccupied with the over-signified Thomson figure and concentrates on Wieland's delineation of the Eulalie character. She presents the feminist issues at stake when a woman is trapped in a patriarchal and bourgeois marriage, and she proposes that the conventions of the melodrama genre are what enabled Wieland to translate a set of feminist issues into cinematic terms: 'Wieland makes the internal contradictions of the family melodrama genre an aesthetic issue. The "subversive" element within the mise-en-scene here becomes the film's dominant way to depict spatial and material entrapment in the family as its primary theme.'[20]

Kay Armatage has written insightfully about Wieland's films as well, and she is responsible for an innovative documentary film on the artist, *Artist on Fire: Joyce Wieland* (1987). Armatage zeroes in on the intersection of feminism and melodrama in a somewhat different way, suggesting that *The Far Shore*'s evocation of a historical moment is enriched by the use of melodrama techniques drawn from the silent-film era (which is exactly the period setting of Wieland's story): 'Although the film is not silent, it employs melodramatic techniques of characterization and narrative common to D.W. Griffith and Jean Vigo.'[21] An important recent text about *The Far Shore* is written by Brenda Longfellow, who takes seriously the feminist aspirations of the film and admires the complexity of the political landscape that Wieland constructs, while also calling attention to the absence of Native peoples in this story, except in coded form. Longfellow remarks, 'Wieland's aesthetic gaze maintains an affinity to Native reverence for the land ... [but] a Native voice is present only in sublimated form through the character of Tom Thomson.'[22]

The Far Shore Today

This book builds on these pre-existing waves of scholarship and proposes that the intersection of landscape and melodrama is crucial for a reappraisal of *The Far Shore*. I therefore address Wieland's film as a key contribution to the debate about landscape and art in Canada, while also recognizing that its idiosyncratic fusion of different genres and media means that *The Far Shore* could be described as a melodramatic landscape film. Indeed, this book sets out to interrogate the circumstances under which landscape and melodrama (as concepts, as genres, as sensibilities) come to be conjoined in Wieland's film. Crucially, as well, *The Far Shore* is considered in relation to Wieland's entire practice as an artist and a filmmaker. Joyce Wieland once stated that her feature-length film would be the culmination of her art practice: '*The Far Shore* was pulling together everything I knew so far in life ... what I knew so far about art.'[23] By the 1970s Wieland had spent two decades exploring painting, assemblage, sculpture, and installation as well as experimental film. Because *The Far Shore* is a feature film, it is entirely possible, of course, to discuss it primarily as such, in relation to filmic genres, in the context of Canadian film history, as a crossover between experimental and commercial film, and so on. But Wieland very adamantly stated that the film was the culmination of her art practice, and this book takes the artist/filmmaker at her word in this respect; I have attempted not to isolate *The Far Shore* because of its medium but rather to regard the film as a genuine manifestation of the artist's inter-media practice.

Chapter 1 provides an overview of Wieland's career as an artist during the 1960s and 1970s, while focusing on how Wieland developed a distinctive cinematic imagination across the multiple media and materials of her art practice. In many paintings, sculptural assemblages, and hand-stitched works of the 1960s, for instance, Wieland explored sequentiality, seriality, and the illusion of movement, often through the explicit use of devices borrowed from the cinema. It was as Wieland was producing such materially varied works that she also began making short experimental films, showing them to a small but influential community of New York-based filmmakers, including Wieland's husband at the time, Michael Snow. Her peripheral involvement with the 'structural film' movement is relevant to this discussion because her filmic production, even while committed to formal and structural experimentation, would inevitably be enlivened through some kind of narrative spark; this is what differentiated her art practice and what apparently made her affiliation with the more hard-core structuralists rather tenuous. Wieland's images and objects from the 1960s and 1970s introduce some element – political allegory, sexual joke, cartoon-like gag, and so on – which can be classified under the rubric of narrative. Some critics have been unable to reconcile the overt formal experimentation of Wieland's short, early films with the conventionality of *The Far Shore*, but in a sense, embarking on a feature-length film allowed her to fully develop the interest in narrative and storytelling that is present in embryonic form in some of her earliest artworks. The strong emphasis on a storyline in *The Far Shore* should not have been so surprising to viewers familiar with the totality of Wieland's career. And although this point was not made at the time, it can be said that Wieland approached the question of narrative with deconstructive zeal and with structural rigour.

It is perhaps Wieland's 1971 bookwork entitled *True Patriot Love / Veritable Amour Patriotique* that best conveys how the artist developed the notion of a proto-cinematic imagination. In this bookwork (sometimes called an 'artist's book') excerpts from a script that would become *The Far Shore* appear for the first time. But not simply the textual traces of a future film-project matter here, because within the pages of this remarkable book a complex 'cinematic' landscape makes its appearance, albeit in fragmented form. There is a sustained tension between still and moving images; the camera is positioned to emphasize an embodied, mobile experience of landscape; there are shifts in emphasis between interior and exterior views, between scenes framed from above or at ground level; and so on. Then, not fully connected to all these pictorial stratagems but rather adjacent to them, the lines of text introduce a few details about the main characters, and this is enough to suggest the narrative and affective momentum that is such an integral part of the cinema. In this way, Wieland's aesthetic inquiry into the constituent parts of a cinematic imagination would lead to the making of *The Far Shore*.

Chapter 2 explicitly takes up the question of landscape, focusing on the Tom character, as I argue that *The Far Shore* critically engages with the Canadian tradition of landscape painting, of which Tom Thomson is an exemplar. It is important to remember, as well, that Wieland's film itself is a work of (cinematic) landscape art, created a couple of generations after Thomson. By the time Wieland came to make *The Far Shore*, her artwork had appropriated and manipulated various signs and symbols of Canadian identity – and the iconic figure of Tom Thomson would be taken up in a similar spirit. Thomson's early death and unfulfilled promise as an artist have accorded him a unique martyr-like status in the cultural history of Canada, as if he died for the cause of Canadian art. Wieland's film offers a new version of this traumatic event; instead of a lone, celibate artist confronting a harsh natural environment, Tom Thomson's landscape art practice is presented in more complex, dialectical terms. We become aware that the significance of landscape is never purely aesthetic, but rather, that it emerges as part of a constellation of forces, related to ecological imperatives, political forces, changing social relations, subjective responses, and so forth. To develop this analysis, I draw on theories of the landscape genre from art history and focus on some recent scholarship pertaining to the figuration of landscape in cinematic terms. By the end of *The Far Shore* it is no longer possible to regard the landscape as a mere backdrop for the story, because the natural environment has become a veritable player in the melodramatic narrative.

The Far Shore implicitly asks: what is the value of Thomson? At the present time that question is easy enough to answer in monetary terms: in May 2008 a small oil sketch, *Pine Trees at Sunset*, sold at auction for almost $2 million, and other characteristically tiny Thomson works have recently sold for comparable amounts. But the question of aesthetic or cultural value is much more difficult to resolve. Wieland seemed to recognize in Thomson a kindred spirit and, to some extent, in *The Far Shore* her vision of landscape merges with his. Through this fusion, we understand that landscape art (and here we can take this term to encompass both Thomson's paintings and Wieland's film) is not merely part of the investment portfolio of Canada's affluent few, nor should it be accepted as an easy symbol of Canadian identity. Images of the land can be powerful; they have the potential to unleash utopian imaginings. Wieland recognizes this emancipatory potential in the landscape vision of Thomson and wants to restore it.

Sherrill Grace's 2004 book, *Inventing Tom Thomson*, inventories a remarkable assortment of stories, scholarly accounts, plays, and pictures of the artist that have appeared over the years. Perhaps we can be sure that Tom Thomson has acquired a mythic stature precisely because the story of his life and death seems to require constant retelling. The man's personality remains enigmatic, and as the exact circumstances of Thomson's death by drowning have never been established, a great deal of speculation, if not overt fictionalizing, has been produced. Grace astutely comments that the death scene in Canoe Lake and the corpse itself have become the objects of obsessive interest: 'His dead body has come to represent a complex narrative web of meaning and associations that rivals, if not overshadows, the body of his work.'[24] Many of the texts reviewed by Grace reveal a forensic fixation on how Thomson died: whether he might have fallen overboard accidentally, whether he might have been assaulted with a blunt instrument, and so on. Wieland, too, replays the death scene for us and, indeed, as the story is set in 1919, two years after the death of the real Thomson, it is as if he has been artificially resuscitated only to die again for a new audience, as it were. Thus, Thomson's spectacularized death accrues in significance, as it is played out in the 1910s, in 1976 when Wieland released her film, and in 2008–9 as I write this text.

Chapter 3 shifts the focus from Tom to Eulalie. If the key term for the preceding chapter is landscape, it is melodrama that now provides the conceptual infrastructure. At one level, the plot of *The Far Shore* is directly informed by the feminist politics of the 1970s, especially regarding the lack of agency for women within the social institution of marriage. Eulalie is trapped in an unhappy marriage, her husband rules the household, and her ability to express herself emotionally and artistically is further curtailed by bourgeois convention. The film focuses on Eulalie's melancholy, artistic frustration and, above all, her desire for Tom; it is the melodramatic contrast between her interior and exterior realities that provides the film with its narrative momentum. Eventually, the protagonist acts: she physically attacks her husband and damages his property before her fateful, fully clothed dive into the lake. In Wieland's revisionist history, it is also made clear that Tom, too, is (melodramatically) in love, and if Eulalie's actions promise to irrevocably change his life and his art, we see that this is his deepest desire as well. Like Eulalie, Tom evidently wants to break through some social or psychic barrier, to achieve some further stage of fulfilment. It is thus that the lonely, frozen image of Tom Thomson that has come down to us is productively destabilized through the affective excess of melodrama.

But *The Far Shore* is not only concerned with Eulalie's emotional life and with re-presenting Tom's relationship to the land; the story is also about how this fictional woman character (who is also an artist in her own right) struggles to connect affectively, imaginatively, and sexually to the land. When Eulalie suddenly dives into the lake , she claims that natural environment as the very site of her own desire: with this powerful image Wieland provided the Canadian public with an explicitly gendered 'figure in a landscape.' In terms of plot she personifies the quest for identity and self-realization, in both personal and collective terms. Here it is important to note that Eulalie occupies a subject-position that is doubly 'other' and place-less: she is a woman without power or property in a patriarchal world, and she is a Québcoise only provisionally situated in Canada, as noted by her Toronto-establishment husband when he says, 'remember one thing, my dear ... you are the foreigner.' This is how I understand Wieland's claim that the political content of her film would be hidden from view behind a very 'romantic' storyline. Wieland very effectively uses melodrama to trigger political effects – a new vision of landscape, a reflection on gender relations, an alternative take on Canadian nationalism.

A Nationalist Film, a National Cinema?

It is a curious coincidence that, whereas Tom Thomson became central to the identification of a national school of painting in the early years of the twentieth century,[25] by the time Joyce Wieland's *The Far Shore* was released in 1976, it was the possible emergence of a national cinema that was a concern, and indeed the cause of some cultural anxiety. In a 1977 publication Peter Harcourt wrote: 'How can we in Canada ... achieve a cinema of our own? What form might it take? Who will be interested in it? And who will pay for it?'[26] The response to Wieland's film was to some extent mired in such musings – about whether a given film was helping to build a national cinema and whether Canadian films were supposed to enhance a sense of national identity. (Judy Steed points out that by this time Quebec was steadily producing high-quality films that genuinely explored history, nationhood, and identity and that she and Wieland understood the 'national crisis' spoken of here to be an English-Canadian one.)[27] Of course, the problems besetting the construction of 'Canadian cinema' are hardly unique; many other countries and communities have faced comparable challenges. About the question of national cinema more generally, Andrew Higson has written: 'To identity a national cinema is first of all to specify a coherence and a unity; it is to proclaim a unique identity and a stable set of meanings. The process of identification is thus invariably a hegemonizing, mythologizing process ... At the same time, the concept of a national cinema has almost invariably been mobilized as a strategy of cultural (and economic) resistance: a means of asserting national autonomy in the face of (usually) Hollywood's international domination.'[28] Higson's twofold definition of national cinema speaks to the case of *The Far Shore*, it seems to me. Wieland deliberately set out to tackle themes and iconographies that pertain to Canadian nationhood, and she unabashedly engaged with that 'mythologizing process' that can result in a 'stable set of meanings,' even while the end result was not meant to be a conciliatory cultural product. At the same time, it can be said that Wieland's film met the expectation that, as a Canadian film, there would be something demonstrably different, something distinctively un-Hollywoodish about its story and style.

Joyce Wieland might not have had the ambition to single-handedly forge a national cinema, but she was certainly committed to the idea that Canadian nationalism had to be renegotiated and that artists and cultural producers of her generation had a responsibility to fulfil in this respect. Retelling the Tom Thomson story during the 1970s was necessary, because this alternative history would resonate with the countercultural and environmental politics then on the rise in Canada. Wieland was intimately connected with the New Left movements of the 1960s and 1970s, and she shared the convictions of Abraham Rotstein, James Laxer, and other public intellectuals, that Canada's national resources were being commodified and sold off with little regard for environmental concerns or the social survival of the people of the north, while Canadian sovereignty was losing out to American concerns.[29] These political commitments are evident in multiple artworks and are voiced repeatedly by Wieland in interviews throughout the 1970s; in other words, there is an intellectual/political formation that coincides with Wieland's revisionist landscape vision. By the 1970s Wieland was warning about a crisis that was ecological in the broadest sense of the term, endangering nature, nation, and psyche. It was thus with a sense of urgency that the artist turned to the past. By replaying the Tom Thomson story in a new way, the present-day crisis would be illuminated.

The Far Shore comes to a tragic end, as the lovers fail to escape and are instead brutally murdered; in this respect we might say that Wieland's story functions as a cautionary tale. Tom and Eulalie fail to gain access to the landscape that has become their mutual object of desire – which raises questions about who really has access to the national territory, whether as profit-making resource, as source of aesthetic inspiration, or as cultural capital. But the 'far shore' of the title of Wieland's film suggests a place that is necessarily regarded from a distance. Indeed, the film sustains a sense of longing (on the part of both Tom and Eulalie) for a distant horizon – a realm of freedom and pleasure that lies beyond the everyday social world, which is somehow embedded in natural places and objects.

Becoming Cinematic

By the time Joyce Wieland decided to make a feature film, she had achieved renown as an experimental filmmaker, and her films were screened and discussed primarily within that specialized context. It is important to recognize, however, that her filmmaking was one component of an art practice that actively forged connections between multiple materials and visual media, including film. In the body of work she created up to *The Far Shore*, it is possible to discern a protracted process of 'becoming cinematic,' through a range of art objects, beyond the actual making of films. Wieland's paintings, collages, sculptural objects, and bookwork show a sustained engagement with cinematic issues such as visual sequentiality and the tension between still and moving images and, crucially, her work again and again introduces narrative.

Wieland's multimedia (or inter-media) practice also needs to be understood as part of a paradigmatic shift in the art world during the 1960s and 1970s. This chapter therefore begins by singling out a few other artists active during this period, who began to explore moving images as part of broader aesthetic trajectories. This focus provides points of comparison for how Wieland came to engage with and problematize a cinematic point of view. I then address Wieland's short experimental films, and the 'structural film' category with which for a time she was associated. It must be emphasized that Wieland's experimentation with film goes beyond questions of perception and medium-specificity. We will see that the distinctive cinematic imagination that evolved in her work was linked to narrative momentum, political storytelling, and the ability to trigger an affective response. And as the script for *The Far Shore* was originally introduced in the form of a structural/conceptual artist's book, entitled *True Patriot Love* (1971), this calls for an extended discussion. *True Patriot Love* announced the forthcoming film and even included fragments of a script for the film, while it could be said that the bookwork itself functions as a proto-film and, more specifically, a proto-landscape-film, in that a sense of visual momentum is created through networks and tracks of images and texts and through the dynamic effect of turning pages, while all of these pictorial qualities are marshalled to evoke a northern landscape. This outline of Wieland's art practice leading up to *The Far Shore* is intended to demonstrate how the 1976 film was a genuine continuation of, and culmination of, Wieland's preoccupations throughout the 1960s and 1970s.

Robert Smithson, Carollee Schneeman, Jack Chambers, Valie Export, and Andy Warhol are only some of the many artists of Wieland's generation who found ways to integrate film – or some kind of moving image – into their art practices. None of them became 'filmmakers' in any exclusive sense of the term, even though some, like Wieland, would be accepted into a distinct world of 'experimental film.' All of these artists made interesting and inventive films, but the circumstances under which they did so varied greatly. Robert Smithson's *Spiral Jetty* (1970) is a telling example of how film would not be regarded as a stand-alone visual medium. The title *Spiral Jetty* encompasses a substantial piece of land art, an essay, and a film, all of which are semantically and aesthetically interconnected. The spiralling arrangement of rocks in Great Salt Lake, Utah, is sculpturally embedded in a pre-existing environment, and the viewer who treads on these rocks must respond phenomenologically to this materiality. Then, Smithson's essay of the same title uses hyberbolic language and literary flourishes to describe the effect of this spiralling motion and to suggest the parameters of a sublime experience. Finally, the film isolates specific moments during the construction, but shifts dramatically from ground-level points of view to aerial views from a helicopter, while this footage is complemented by additional (still) shots of maps, books, dioramas, illustrations, and so on. Thus, the accumulated segments of this artwork produce a reflection on nature, technology, embodiment, and time in which the moving image plays a certain role.

In a very different way, Carollee Schneeman used film to complement her experimentation with painting, sculpture, and performance. The films *Meat Joy* (1964) and *Fuses* (1967) incorporate all of these art forms, while film itself becomes the means to introduce temporal discontinuity, and techniques of close-ups and cropping allow for a shifting visual access to the bodies on display. The case of Jack Chambers also is unique, as he cultivated a realist painting practice even while making films. When describing the effect of temporality he was aiming for, he referred to those paintings as 'instant movies.'[1] If the problem for Chambers was how to make paintings that evoke a temporal dimension, in films such as *Circle* (1969) he played with the conventional cinematic illusionism of time passing; in this case the film consists of pieced-together footage of his own backyard, shot for a few minutes each day over the course of a year. Another interesting body of work was created by the Austrian artist and filmmaker Valie Export, who has been directly compared to Joyce Wieland because both artists 'combined rigorously conceived formal structures with political content.'[2] Another common thread between Wieland and Export is that 1976 was the year both women released feature-length narrative films, after having established themselves as makers of short, experimental films; while Wieland borrowed from the genre of melodrama, Export's *Invisible Adversaries* was a twist on conventional science-fiction films.

It is evident that many artists of this generation recognized the centrality of screens and moving images within contemporary culture and were determined to engage with this dominant form of visual experience. It is worth noting that in 1965 Andy Warhol announced his intention to cease painting in order to devote himself exclusively to the filmmaking career that he had begun in 1963.[3] In fact, he did not abandon painting, but it is still fascinating that he felt the need to dramatically renounce it (as a retrograde visual technology? as an inevitably commodified art form?) in favour of a more truly up-to-date form of picture-making. If some of the artists mentioned above did continue to paint (including Wieland as well as Warhol), the practice of painting would no longer be regarded as a purified, rarified, medium-specific activity. Instead, some of the most compelling artworks produced by these artists suggest points of convergence and friction between painting, cinema, performance, sculpture, crafted objects, mass-produced objects, and so on.

Wieland's Trajectory as an Artist

Wieland did achieve recognition as a painter early in her career, with well-received exhibitions at the Isaacs Gallery in Toronto, beginning in 1960. Like many other artists active in the middle years of the twentieth century, her commitment to a modern form of visuality was initially bound up with abstraction. Artists of various appellations (Abstract Expressionist or Colour-field, for example) were grappling with the questions of whether painting should be figurative or abstract, whether the illusion of three-dimensional space should be replaced with an insistently flat surface, whether the composition should be rationally determined or arrived at through intuitive and unconscious means. The oil painting *Redgasm* from 1960 indicates how Wieland proposed to solve some of these 'problems' posed by abstraction. Clusters of dynamic shapes suggest directional flows of colour and energy, but one of *Redgasm*'s blue spheres is discreetly labelled 'me,' while interspersed among the shapes are lightly scrawled arrows and phallic shapes. These few elements make the viewer aware that this picture cannot be categorized as an abstract painting; it took only a few graffiti-like elements to suggest that the whirling shapes might be describing the unpredictable flow of sexual desire. Thus, the artist's interest in the rudimentary structure of narrative arises very early in her artistic production.

In 1963 Joyce Wieland moved to New York City, where she would reside throughout the decade. The turn away from abstraction, which was already immanent in her practice, would then develop into a committed embrace of figuration and narrative. Indeed, her art practice flourished as she experimented with a wealth of materials and connected with some of the lively art currents of the 1960s – Pop and Conceptual art in particular. Wieland's 'pop' sensibility comes across in many paintings from 1963 (a remarkably productive year for the artist). In paintings such as *Brad's Bridge* and *The Battery*, she used a gridded structure to display heterogeneous elements of everyday city life: individual letters, a dollar sign, a cartoony head, a car – all painted in an abbreviated style associated with advertisements or comic strips. One can imagine the artist on the streets of New York, observing the entertaining parade of gestures, looks, and signage, which become in her paintings a kind of urban code to be deciphered. As was the case for many other artists of the time, the return to figuration coincided with an interest in pop culture: the paintings from this period are brightly coloured, with strong shapes and textual elements, and they share the immediate visual appeal of ads, commercial signage, cartoons, and movies.

More specifically, there is a strong emphasis on cinematic and animation-like effects, across Wieland's production of paintings and hanging assemblages from the mid-1960s. In the aforementioned gridded paintings, where each box contains a different image or sign, the viewer might begin to look at one frame after another, imagining stories that could emerge if the squares were to be shuffled. Very quickly, though, Wieland began work on paintings that are clearly meant to be read sequentially, and where something does indeed seem to happen as we follow the boxed imagery from left to right or from top to bottom.

Sailing is a long, vertically oriented painting divided into seven box-like frames. In the uppermost frame a small boat is seen in the vicinity of a distant horizon, surrounded by water, while the next frame down operates like a jumpcut, so that the sailboat is now apparently closer to the viewer, in the middle ground. The next few frames show the boat as it seemingly moves horizontally across the space. This regular 'movement' is replaced, in the second-to-last frame, by a sudden close-up view of the boat capsizing. The last framed image shows the sailboat almost entirely submerged, with only two small white triangles (the tops of the sails) protruding from an expanse of blue pigment. Wieland would produce many variations of this painting; *Sink* is another such vertical canvas, this time featuring a large ship looming in the foreground, which seems to gradually move out of the picture frame to the left, only to reappear as a small distant object in the last few frames and ultimately to sink beneath the waves. In all of the paintings that are variations on this theme, the inevitable, inexorable disaster ending provides the artworks with a strong narrative logic, despite their cartoon-like simplicity.

This long, vertical format is non-traditional for a painting, but it corresponds to a strip of celluloid with its sequence of still images that will be fed through a machine to create the illusion of movement. There is no doubt that Wieland was deliberately imitating film, as the titles of many such paintings are quite clear: *First integrated film with a short on sailing*, *Four Films*, and *Boat: Homage to D.W. Griffith*, all produced in 1963, as before. All of these film-paintings manage to be both funny and genuinely innovative in their exploration, in painterly terms, of cinematic movement and narrative. *Boat: Homage to D.W. Griffith* shows yet another ship, once again 'moving' through the frame of the picture, from right to left, without a disastrous ending to create narrative closure, but this time the sequence of images is punctuated by an iris-shot – a perfectly spherical framing device – of the boat. It is the adaptation of this iris device that is the painter's homage to Griffith; it constitutes the artist's acknowledgment that the history of the cinema has changed modes of perception and representation. As Marnie Fleming has commented about Wieland's series of film-paintings: 'Progressive visual readings are constantly interrupted by zooms or fades or jump cuts or insert shots, cinematic devices that normally do not hamper the narrative but rather dramatize it.'[4]

What is at stake here is indeed narrative – how it is produced in cinematic terms, and whether it is translatable into other media. However rudimentary the 'story' of these boats passing or sinking might be, Wieland takes for granted that we (twentieth- century viewers) fully accept the multiple viewpoints, shifting perspectives, and pictorial distortions of the cinematic apparatus in the telling of a story. Realism in the cinema is a complex illusion created through a set of strategies, including flashback and cross-cutting, for which Griffith is also renowned. We might also consider such paintings to be a homage to early film because they are 'silent movies' and as such must rely more explicitly on pictorial qualities to tell a story.

Wieland was clearly interested in how stories can be told in a film-like manner. All the paintings discussed so far tell the same rather ridiculous story of a boat suddenly sinking, but despite the cartoony simplicity of the painting style, and despite the repetition of the same scenario, the viewer is quite likely to respond emotionally at the final image of a boat sinking beneath the waves. In other words, the abrupt ending turns the story into a tragedy and, before we know it, we have begun to imaginatively flesh out the contours of a more complex narrative. Nor is it a coincidence that Wieland's arrival in the United States coincides with these 'disaster' paintings. She would later comment about spectacularized violence in the United States, that 'part of the power here is the tradition of sensationalism.'[5] It is also interesting that Andy Warhol was at this very time making paintings based on newspaper coverage of traffic accidents, mass food poisonings, and other such everyday disasters.

Wieland's simple motif of sinking ships allowed her to embark on a formal exploration of 'moving' images, while numerous artworks would emphasize that cinematic sequentiality can be driven by a desire for narrative closure. The painting *West 4th*, for example, has two vertical sequences of images of close-up mouths holding cigarettes that seem to bob up and down, even as the mouths get larger and smaller, as if a camera were zooming in and out on a conversation between two people that might well culminate in an erotic encounter. *First integrated film with a short on sailing* (fig. 1.1) is one of the most complex works from this series. There are two simultaneously unfolding narrative trajectories here – one running horizontally and one vertically. The smaller-scale horizontal sequence of images starts off as the now familiar story of a sailboat happily bobbing along on the surface of a watery expanse, which, instead of ending in disaster, segues into the silhouette of a woman, the outline of a man's head and then some cartoon speech balloons, one of them containing the words 'Oh Walt!' The more prominent 'film' in this painting, however, is the so-called first integrated film, consisting of three vertically stacked frames: the first shows the profiles of a white woman and a black man on the verge of kissing, with little hearts floating between them in case we need a clue about the nature of their physical proximity; the second frame shows them closer together by a millimetre or two; in the last frame they are kissing, although what is made visible is essentially a large yellow blob of the woman's hair and a large area of dark-brown hair and skin. Both

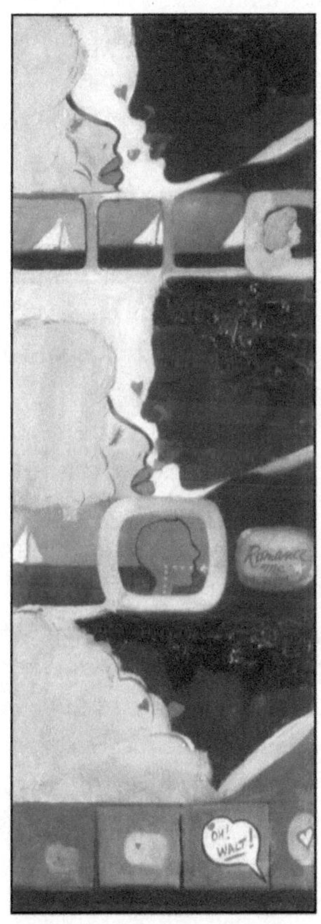

1.1. Joyce Wieland, **First Integrated Film with a Short on Sailing**, 1963 (oil on canvas, 66 × 22.7 cm). National Gallery of Canada, Library and Archives, Ottawa.

'films' thus seem to tell the same kind of story, which is not a tragedy but a comedy, ending as expected with a romantic kiss.

The conventional form of narrative closure that Wieland taps into here is the sublime dissolve between two individuals just before the credits roll – the kiss that vanquishes all obstacles, the kiss that signifies the end of the movie and of the narrative, but that is also the implicit prelude to a future opening up for the individuals concerned, except that the artist also calls attention to the ideological contradictions in American society that make such a conciliatory climax improbable. For, while countless Hollywood films have indeed ended with a close-up of the protagonists embracing, the 'integrated' or interracial kiss was (and still is) a rarity on the big and small screens of America; and if the 'Walt' referred to in the cartoon speech balloon is Walt Disney, this evokes the ostensibly wholesome world of family entertainment that entirely avoids such 'controversial' subject matter.

Putting aside for a moment the narrative content of *First integrated film with a short on sailing*, we see that what is equally interesting is its device of simultaneously occurring horizontal and vertical storylines. This serves to point out the inevitable limitations of both painting and cinema: if it is true that the illusion of cinematic movement is only crudely mimicked in this painting, on the other hand the medium of paint on canvas can easily accommodate two narrative trajectories 'moving' in different directions within the same frame, whereas shorts and features would normally have to succeed each other temporally on-screen.[6] Thus, Wieland's artwork stages an encounter between these two important perceptual and pictorial modes, as if something were to be gained, aesthetically speaking, from this confrontation and the resulting pictorial hybridity.

Many of Wieland's multimedia sculptural assemblages of the mid-1960s were also organized in such a way as to mimic the shape of the vertical filmic strip – although in these cases there is less emphasis on narrative momentum. *Stuffed Movie* (1966), for instance, consists of clear plastic envelopes that have been stitched together, enclosing bits of photographs, newspaper clippings, and personal mementoes. Another work with a similar format and sensibility is called *War and Peace: 8 mm Home Movie* (1966): in this case the plastic in question is a hot pink colour, and one can discern only with difficulty the references to the Vietnam War on the newspaper clippings folded and sealed inside. With this extensive use of plastic, it was not only the iconography or subject matter of pop culture that the artist appropriated, but its distinctive material qualities – the gloss, the reflective surfaces, the expendibility. If Wieland called these artworks movies, our spectatorship of the assemblages is only obliquely movie-like. The objects and figures appearing inside the frames are of different sizes, which in filmic terms could mean they are seen either up close or from a distance, while their juxtaposition within the same sequence could be akin to filmic montage. However, for such sculptural objects, it is the assertive materiality of these movie-objects that stands out, in marked contrast to the dematerialized projected image of the real movies. What I have been addressing, with these examples of Wieland's non-filmic art practice of the mid-1960s, is how the artist explored the 'cinematic' through a range of media, both before and after she actually began making films.

Experimental Filmmaking

During the 1950s in Toronto, Wieland worked for a time for a company that made documentary and animated films; there she acquired the requisite set of skills related to filmmaking.[7] Although she apparently did experiment a bit with film at the time, it was the move to New York that triggered her commitment to this medium. Indeed, Wieland became involved in the avant-garde/experimental film scene in New York City soon after her arrival. If she did not become similarly ensconced in a visual-art community, it must be acknowledged that New York's institutional network of galleries, museums, dealers, and collectors was not easy to penetrate. The people who were making and showing experimental films were, in comparison, much more loosely organized and affiliated and more welcoming. Wieland began attending the midnight screenings of experimental films put on by Jonas Mekas and became friendly with many of the participants, including Shirley Clarke, Hollis Frampton, the brothers George and Mike Kuchar – all of whom she would collaborate with at some point.

It was a screening of Jack Smith's *Flaming Creatures* (1963) that seemed to make the biggest impression on Wieland: she would later comment, 'when I saw *Flaming Creatures* something went "pop" ... it was the biggest release to know that that was possible.'[8] Wieland does not explain in much detail what she admired in Smith's film, but *Flaming Creatures* was extraordinary for its improvisational elements, do-it-yourself exoticism, and casually aberrant sexuality; just as impressive, perhaps, was that such a film had been made on a miniscule budget. *Flaming Creatures* was also an experimental film endowed with a narrative of sorts and, indeed, Jack Smith was adamant about the importance of stories.[9] Wieland's first efforts with film included some humorous stop-motion productions such as *Patriotism* (1964), which features a kind of rude parade with American flags and hotdogs. She then went on to make short films such as *Water Sark* (1965), where the artist is situated in her New York studio/home and approaches the interaction with everyday things, and with her own body, as a perceptual experiment; *Hand Tinting* (1967), made from leftover footage from a documentary about African-American girls, which strategically isolates gesture and body movement; *Sailboat* (1967), which uses the realism of film as a counterpoint to all those cartoon-like paintings of sinking ships. These and other films were well received, and after *Rat Life and Diet in North America* (1968) and *Reason Over Passion* (1969) appeared, Wieland's sophistication as a filmmaker was widely acknowledged. The *Village Voice*'s Andrew Sarris indicated the extent to which she had become recognized and admired, when he wrote in 1971: 'the talented Canadian Joyce Wieland leads the contingent of women film-makers in the experimental, abstract, poetic, avant-garde, underground categories.'[10]

It is certainly impressive that within a few years this erstwhile Canadian painter would contribute so much to the American experimental film scene. 'Experimental, abstract, poetic': Sarris provides a list of categories that Wieland supposedly tops, but one category that is strikingly absent from his appraisal is the 'structural' designation. Nonetheless, Wieland was associated with structural film on many occasions and then defined against it, so it is important to examine the parameters of this movement, which achieved coherence both in the United States and in the United Kingdom. As a branch of experimental film, the structural impulse was quite deliberately positioned against the illusionism, narrative ploys, processes of identification, and emotional cues of mainstream cinema. For the filmmaker and theorist of structural film Peter Gidal all of these characteristics of the conventional cinema were 'ideological strangleholds.' Instead, he argued, 'the Structural/Materialist film must minimise the content in its overpowering, imagistically seductive sense, in an attempt to get through this miasmic area of "experience" and proceed with film as film.'[11]

So it would be 'film as film,' that is, the formal, material, and structural qualities of cinema, that was ostensibly brought forward by filmmakers. Another influential author, P. Adams Sitney, writing in 1969 about the new tendency he detected within the world of experimental film, would announce: 'Suddenly, a cinema of structure has emerged.' At this point, Sitney located Wieland squarely within this movement: 'Tony Conrad, George Landow, Michael Snow, Hollis Frampton, Joyce Wieland, Ernie Gehr, and Paul Sharits have produced a number of remarkable films ... theirs is a cinema of structure wherein the shape of the whole film is predetermined and simplified, and it is that shape that is the primal impression of the film.'[12] Many of Wieland's films do share typically structuralist concerns such as the separation of sound and image, the use of non-naturalistic repetition, and the strategic heightening of one aspect of the cinematic experience at the expense of others. Wieland's film *Sailboat* is a good example of this constellation of interests. As it is also a film that apparently takes up where the sinking-ship filmstrip paintings left off, we can trace the intersection between these different moments of her art practice. The word *sailboat* superimposed over the moving image immediately serves to interrupt the naturalism of the representation. Over a three-minute period a boat repeatedly crosses the screen, although the viewer is discouraged from thinking this movement implies a passage of time because of discrepancies in the length of each shot. Gradually, the boat seems to disappear into the very graininess of the filmic image. As Bart Testa has commented about *Sailboat*, 'the montage and almost painterly atmospheric effects of this film are much softer than her film-like still works.'[13]

Eventually, though, many commentators came to recognize something in Wieland's work that made her a less than perfect fit with structural film. Only one year after claiming her for the nascent structuralist initiative, Sitney would write about Wieland, 'Formally her films owe allegiance to the structuralists, yet what is happening on the screen, moment by moment, is quite different.'[14] The 'difference' Sitney points to was actually alluded to in his earlier text, when he remarked, 'in Sailboat, the structural principle is clearly ironic.'[15] Wieland's films are indeed permeated by irony and humour, and it is quite evident that the spectre of narrative has not been entirely expunged from her sensibility. To encounter the structuralists' extreme bias against narrative, one need look no further than statements by Michael Snow (Wieland's husband): 'I am interested in exploring sound image relations that are structural and have little or nothing to do with reinforcing narrative (i.e., this is sad, this is funny, this is exciting, etc.)'[16] Despite such rhetoric, Snow's practice as a filmmaker and visual artist has at times addressed the seductive power of narrative, perhaps most famously in the otherwise high-structural film *Wavelength* (1967), where the space of a room is slowly traversed by a camera. But this inexorable movement is interrupted by a few actions sufficient to suggest a world of narrative intrigue occurring in adjacent spaces, off-screen and behind the scenes. Joyce Wieland's artwork and films are more directly, and more consistently, committed to exploring the structural complexity and emotive power of narrative – even if this means returning to the scene of the crime, as it were – the commercial cinema of genres. Wieland's ultimate solution was to make a film that included melodramatic characters and plotlines, but that also evoked the narrative simplicity of myth or fable, and that incorporated sequences of barely moving images. Nor was Wieland the only experimental filmmaker to come full circle in this way, as in the 1970s Laura Mulvey, Peter Wollen, Valie Export, and Sally Potter, for instance, all attempted to reappropriate and reinvent the narrative feature film, even while they approached this challenge in very different ways.[17]

The fourteen-minute film *Rat Life and Diet in North America* can be regarded as a bridge between Wieland's experimental shorts and the eventual undertaking of a feature-length narrative film. This remarkable film shows close-up views of Wieland's pet gerbils (playing the role of rats), introduced into different *mises en scène*: next to a window, on a street, on a tabletop filled with dishes and food, in a meadow filled with flowers and fruit (fig. 1.2). Through the use of inter-titles and words superimposed over the images, this sequence of cute tableaux becomes the story of political prisoners in the United States who escape their persecutors and cross the border into Canada, where they intend to become organic farmers, except that the United States invades Canada

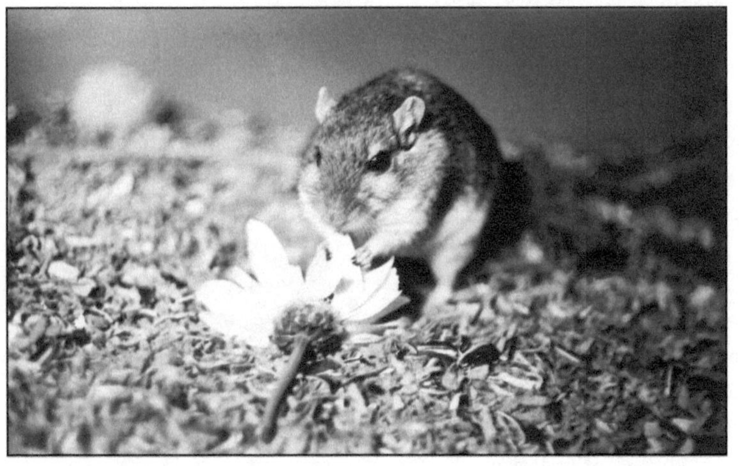

1.2. Joyce Wieland, **Rat Life and Diet in North America**, 1968 (still image from 14-minute colour film). National Gallery of Canada, Library and Archives, Ottawa.

– at which point the film ends with a thudding sound. The film's sense of dramatic urgency is enhanced through a musical soundtrack that shifts in mood, through crescendos of sound effects, while the jittery animals quite 'naturally' contribute to the sense of paranoia suggested by the storyline.

One of the most criticized aspects of mainstream cinema, for structuralists, was the idea that a filmmaker's role is to create characters with whom the viewing audience will then identify. For theorists such as Gidal this process of identification was to be avoided, because it inevitably locked the viewer into a position of passive consumption: 'The commercial cinema could not do without the mechanism of identification. It is the cinema of consumption, in which the viewer is of necessity not a producer of ideas, of knowledge.'[18] Yet it can be argued that *Rat Life and Diet in North America* manages to have it both ways, providing characters to identify with, but also acknowledging the absurdity of identifying with rodent-heroes. Yet this parody of cinematic heroism does ask the audience to reflect on persecution by the state and the quest for freedom; viewers of the film are asked to become producers of knowledge, in Gidal's terms.

Of course, this rudimentary narrative was intelligible to circa-1968 viewers because it corresponded to the historical upheavals of the 1960s. The rodent-protagonists recall the many thousands of opponents to the Vietnam War who fled across the border to Canada. So *Rat Life and Diet in North America* is different from contemporaneous structural films not because Wieland showed she had forsaken a rigorous formal analysis of film, but because this level of aesthetic investigation was overlaid with heroic characters, narrative, allegory, humour, and politics. Another quality of the film that must be noted is its fusion of narrative and politics to landscape aesthetics; as a reconfiguration of the landscape genre, *Rat Life and Diet and North America* can be directly linked to *The Far Shore*.

The *True Patriot Love* Bookwork and the Illusion of Movement

Up to this point I have discussed how Joyce Wieland's artworks staged an aesthetic dialogue between still and moving images, and in this respect, I have suggested, Wieland was at the forefront of a new generation of artists. We have seen that paintings could be movie-like, even while the temporal flow of filmic images is called into question. The artwork that is most strikingly situated at the threshold between visual media, between stillness and movement, is the bookwork entitled *True Patriot Love*. In this artwork the reader learns about a feature film, through the matter-of-fact insertion of script fragments. The title accorded to the film in the book directly echoes that of the exhibition, with the addition of a subtitle, 'True Patriot Love: A Canadian Love, Technology, Leadership and Art Story,' immediately identified as 'A movie by Joyce Wieland.' But the book not only announces a future project, as its experimental accumulation of texts and images itself is informed by a cinematic imagination. In a way, the *True Patriot Love* book offers a glimpse of a film that was never made, the kind of film *The Far Shore* might have been.

It was as part of her solo exhibition at the National Gallery of Canada in 1971 that Wieland produced this bookwork, available for purchase as if it were the exhibition catalogue. She used a government publication about Arctic flowers as a kind of scrapbook, so that the simple line drawings, maps, and dry scientific prose of the original book are interrupted and sometimes obliterated by a display of black-and-white photographs and textual material. This material is attached to the book with pins and paper clips, or sometimes stitched to the page (since Wieland's hand-made manuscript was reproduced for the exhibition, the pins and stitches appear photographically.)

The significance of the film project at this stage of its realization was intimately linked to the exhibition and its interrelated objects, words, images, events, and performative gestures. Many of the individual artworks in *True Patriot Love* overtly addressed the theme of nationhood, while overall there was an emphasis on nature, the land, and the North. Wieland intervened in the discourse about Canadian identity by re-presenting official iconography in idiosyncratic, satirical, and sometimes angry ways. The maple leaf flag appears throughout the exhibition in many different incarnations: for instance, in knitted, stretched-out shapes; as botanical specimen; as part of a photographed performance. The national anthem, heraldic animals such as the beaver, and a certain type of uninhabited-landscape picture also were recurring motifs. There were few paintings in this exhibition, moreover, as the artworks hanging painting-like on walls were likely to be embroidered, stitched, knitted, and/or quilted. With this exhibition Wieland showed that it was possible (and necessary!) to claim, reappropriate, and imaginatively transform the symbolic architecture of Canadian identity. This was no simple affirmation of patriotism. For Wieland, 'true patriotic love' would not be achieved without a process of ideological and political struggle. A warning about 'U.S. technological imperialism' is half-hidden in one artwork, while one of her most trenchant political artworks from this exhibition, *Water Quilt*, called attention to the commodification of water and other natural resources. It could be said that Wieland's *True Patriot Love* exhibition functioned as a kind of exhortation to her fellow citizens to follow her example, by not taking for granted the state's monopoly over such images and icons, and instead becoming actively involved – materially, aesthetically, politically – with the unfinished process of becoming Canadian. As we will see, this attitude would be carried over to Wieland's treatment of Tom Thomson, in the book and subsequently in *The Far Shore*. As a Canadian symbol of sorts, the meaning of 'Thomson' is not regarded as something fixed or reified, but rather, the artist-icon is made available for reconfigured national desires.

The *True Patriot Love* book did include a list of works and other such practical information, on separate booklets tucked into the back of the book, but otherwise the usual features of an exhibition catalogue were largely absent from this publication. There was no essay to explicate the artwork, and while photographic reproductions of artworks in the exhibition did appear throughout the pages of the book, it was at best an eccentric documentation project, focusing on small details or blurring specific objects beyond recognition; nor are the images consistently labelled or otherwise identified. In Wieland's bookwork, her own artworks are de-familiarized through this translation into a new medium.

Wieland's 'pop' sensibility was mentioned earlier, although even artworks such as the sinking-ship paintings, while quite comic-like, show a conceptual rigour. The *True Patriot Love* book has been recognized, in fact, as a significant contribution to Conceptual Art.[19] Wieland's anti-catalogue bookwork does not perform the usual museological functions, which is in keeping with how many Conceptual artists questioned the role of museums as mechanisms of validation and authentication, with the power to endow value on select precious objects. Also, the *True Patriot Love* book brings together multiple forms of signifying stystems – photographs, drawings, maps, printed text, handwriting, and so on – and this convergence, too, is important. Benjamin Buchloh has suggested that Conceptual Art's emphasis on language was a way of undermining the 'status of the object: its visuality, its commodity status, and its form of distribution.'[20] Although a minority of Conceptually oriented artists would focus exclusively on language, Wieland was among many of her generation to consistently work across the domains of the pictorial and the linguistic. Certainly, language was enormously important to Wieland's project as a whole at the National Gallery, while the bookwork in particular is a complex conglomeration of different textual components, which weaves around and through the images. In addition, visually comparable to the printed text or handwriting are various instances of cryptic marks: stitches crossing a page, the pattern of snowshoe tracks, the punctuation of a paper clip. Further, it could be said that Wieland's partial photographs of her own artworks become an entirely new archive of signs, to be recombined in new sequences. Wieland's book has a 'linguistic' logic in the sense that texts, images, and other forms of mark-making appear as fragmented units of meaning, which have the potential to be aligned and 'read' in different ways. This act of reading, in turn, suggests a kind of virtual movement through a sequence of social and natural spaces.

Wieland's book deployed multiple strategies to suggest cinematic-like movement. To some extent she merely enhanced the structural properties of all books, which is to say that a temporal dimension is achieved by the gradual turning of pages. Also, throughout the publication, many images are laid out in black-bordered strips, suggestive once again of the building-blocks of filmic movement. In addition, many of the photographic images appearing in the book have the kind of blur that suggests they were taken by bodies or machines in motion.

As was the case with some of the artwork discussed earlier in this chapter, here, too, Wieland used narrative to affectively involve the viewer/reader and thus to provide a certain structural momentum. This particular aspect of her practice corresponds to a proposition by Guiliana Bruno, regarding the apprehension of still images. In a discussion of filmic and artistic projects including both Gerhard Richter's *Atlas* project (a personal archive of still images) and Chris Marker's *La Jetée* (a film composed of still images), Bruno says that the 'moving effect' of these works encompasses both senses of the word moving: motion and emotion. She argues that under certain circumstances an arrangement of still images can be galvanized and set in motion; it happens when we encounter a storyline that affects us, that moves us: 'pictures are transformed into narratives by way of emotive mobilization.'[21] This rings true in the case of Wieland's *True Patriot Love* book, as the reader/viewer is initially bombarded with images that are fractured and semantically adrift, but forty pages or so into the book, when a few selections from a script are introduced, everything changes. Suddenly the bookwork acquires narratological and affective momentum, and that backlog of fragmented visual information is just as suddenly invested with new meaning as it becomes anchored to the storyline.

In the first part of the book there are details of artworks, close-ups of hands sewing, landscape views, and other close-ups of snowshoe tracks, along with various textual items about the North, including the original book's discussion of botanical specimens and their ecosystems, the handwritten story of an Eskimo woman who becomes a shaman, and a newspaper clipping reporting on a visit to the Arctic by the U.S. secretary of state; in other words, scientific knowledge, spiritual beliefs, and geopolitical events are juxtaposed. The title of the film and other script fragments then begin to appear in snapshot form, within the same square shape and white border as other photographs in the book do. These pieces of the script were photographed from slightly oblique angles, blurring or cutting off edges of words, and the lines of text also appear in different sizes through the succeeding pages, as if the manuscript itself has been subject to a mobile (erratic even) camera, moving closer and then away. Moreover, these snapshots of script fragments overlap on the page, further ensuring that our reading can be only partial. Yet the main protagonists of the story, Tom and Eulalie, are clearly announced, and on the following pages grainy photographs of a standing man and a woman's face serve to further solidify these personages.

Some pages further, Tom Thomson's well-known painting *The West Wind* appears five times, as if on a contact sheet or strip of film (fig. 1.3). As was the case with the script fragments, here the painting (or rather, its reproduction, since a printed caption is apparent in two frames) has been photographed from different angles, resulting in a variable light striking it. Thus, temporality and movement are introduced into

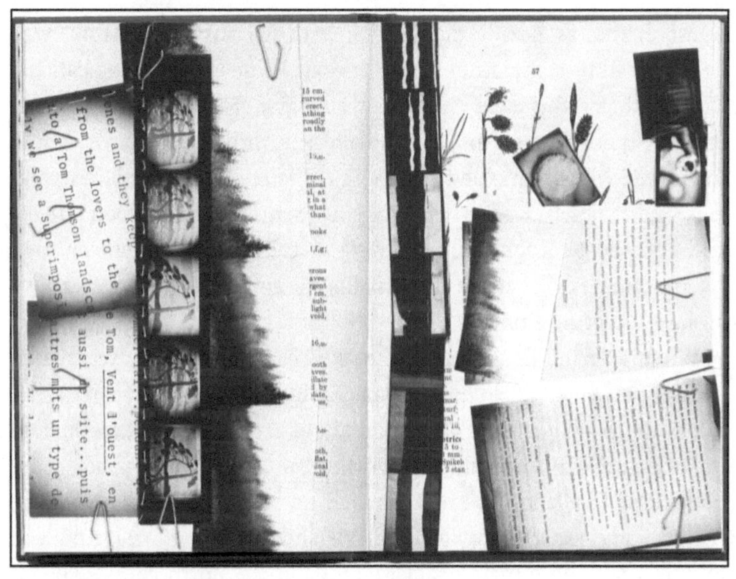

1.3. Joyce Wieland, **True Patriot Love bookwork**, 1971. National Gallery of Canada, Library and Archives, Ottawa.

the representation of the iconic paintings.[22] These pages encapsulate Wieland's way of introducing narrative as one thread within a conglomeration of material transformations and distortions.

It is impossible to grasp the full extent of the story from the fragments of script included in the bookwork, because they are few in number, and, as already mentioned, even what is shown is likely to be obscured by some other image or text. There are some indications, though, that at this stage Wieland was imagining a more fantastical cinematic experiment: for instance, Eulalie is described as a woman who is infatuated with technology, and there are references to airplanes, cameras, and radios, as well as anachronistic mentions of television screens and Polaroid photographs. According to the script fragment entitled 'Scene One,' 'Eulalie stares at the radio, the small dial on it comes alive and we ... picture a tiny t.v.'[23]

When Wieland finally came to make *The Far Shore* some years later, she decided against such non-naturalistic interruptions of the narrative. But perhaps what is most important about the *True Patriot Love* book in relation to the finished film is how the Tom and Eulalie characters are embedded in a landscape that is made up of a network of ecological, political, and artistic storylines. In Wieland's book we are introduced to a 'movie' whose main characters inhabit the north country, but it is significant that Wieland has by this point already made us aware of presences, voices, and gazes criss-crossing the northern terrain and continually intersecting with natural ecosystems. Whatever story these characters are caught up in will take place deep inside this landscape. And if the book does provide a proto-cinematic perspective in relation to them, it is in the sense of accounting for multiple, and intersecting points of view.

It can be argued that *The Far Shore* inverts the narratological structure of the *True Patriot Love* bookwork. If the story (the affective momentum) arrives late in the book and provides only a faint narrative stirring within the rigorously structured arrangement of words and pictures, the film instead delivers a large dose of sentiment right from the beginning and goes on to provide ever intense flashes of desire, melancholy, anger, and lust. Out of all the kinds of narrative possible, Wieland chose the melodrama, where the affective dimension never lets up; it takes over.

The Far Shore in Development

After conceiving of a filmic dimension for her bookwork, Wieland worked on the script for *The Far Shore* throughout the early 1970s, and eventually her old friend Brian Barney was asked to help her to refine the script. Yet alongside this script development, she cultivated the visual aspect of the film as a distinct project. Two years after the film was released, in fact, Pierre Théberge, curator at the National Gallery of Canada, organized a touring exhibition of the the sketches and storyboards Wieland assiduously worked on in the years leading up to the making of the film. Some of these drawings are simple but vigorous black-and-white pencil sketches, while others are more carefully worked up with coloured pencils; indeed, some sequences of these more finished drawings are reminiscent of more recent experiments with the comix/graphic-novel genre. Inscribed on, around, or alongside these drawn elements, Wieland added a wealth of scribbled comments related to the construction of individual shots. As Théberge commented, 'Wieland used the series of drawings to prepare whole filmed sequences, as well as to study camera angles, colour combinations, actors' gestures, setting, etc.'[24] While some filmmakers (perhaps Alfred Hitchcock most famously) are known to have used storyboarding to ensure visual control, what makes this case more unusual is that the director herself was responsible for making these drawings. This body of work makes it evident that Wieland conceived of her 'moving picture' as an extension of her drawing and sketching practice; the collection of still images would eventually begin to move. On the occasion of the exhibition of the drawings for *The Far Shore* in 1978 the journalist Susanne Tausig remarked: 'as the preparatory sketches and film reveal, she treats each individual shot as a separate composition.'[25] If *The Far Shore* can be characterized as a slow-moving film, this is to say that we are obliged to look at still, or almost still, images for quite a long time. The pictures move, but they have maintained something of their identity as still images. Drawing once more on Bruno's idea of 'emotive mobilization,' we might say that movement does not happen gratuitously, but rather that the transition from stillness to motion occurs for specific (affective) reasons.

The interest in narrative structure that Wieland had sustained throughout various projects, and across different materials and media would be developed most fully in *The Far Shore*. A range of cinematic devices and pictoral strategies is used to construct a narrative, including the repetition of certain motifs, figurations, and gestures; characteristically slow camera movements; and distinctive edits and dissolves. But above all it is melodrama that provides the film with its narrative structure: the first hour or so of the film moves slowly and deliberately from one scenario to the next, but the pace and emotional tone of the last part of the film are quite different, as the storylines propelling these characters eventually collide in staccato episodes of lust, anger, and violence. All the action of the film then takes place quickly, even confusedly. Every tension – kept melodramatically taut until now – surfaces and erupts. And it is crucial that these final explosive scenes take place once all the main characters have relocated to the 'north country.'

Some criticism of *The Far Shore* pertained to how Wieland apparently 'broke from ... the avant-garde' with this film.[26] This assessment perhaps is true in certain respects, but does such a break constitute a betrayal? Certainly Wieland seemed to aspire to narrative complexity and cohesion, and she mimicked mainstream modes of spectatorial identification, in order to elicit strong emotional responses. All of these qualities had been subject to critique by some avant-gardists of Wieland's generation. But this is not to say that *The Far Shore* lacks self-reflexivity and levels of formal experimentation. We have seen how narrative structure was problematized throughout her artistic practice and became central to her feature film. But I am arguing that, above all, *The Far Shore* is a complex engagement with the structure and semantics of the landscape genre, understood as a foundational category within the history of art. Many questions that have preoccupied both artists and theorists of art regarding landscape are taken up by the filmmaker; so *The Far Shore* reconsiders the framing and spatialization of natural environments, figure/ground relations, and the pictorial representation of ephemeral natural phenomena. The film as a whole is attuned to the meaning of landscape, insofar as this genre asks us to consider how natural sites come up against human culture, how natural phenomena can become metaphor or allegory, how nature enters into a modern consciousness, and so forth. Wieland's film can also be thought of as an ecological landscape picture, in terms that are comparable to Félix Guattari's concept of 'three ecologies,' whereby the environment, the social formation, and the human psyche are understood to be three interlocked and continually interacting ecosystems.[27] The landscape component of the film is what might have offered, more conventionally, a respite from urban bustle and from the camera's constant movement; landscape imagery might have provided some moments of stillness and contemplation. But *The Far Shore* does provide us with a 'moving landscape,' a landscape that moves because it is part of human history and because, by the end of the film, the natural environment is thoroughly imbued with pathos.

Landscape and Narrative (Tom)

Eighty minutes or so into *The Far Shore*, the viewer is finally rewarded with an image of Tom perched on the bank of a lake, painting a small picture (fig. 2.1). This scene provides a moment of historical verisimilitude, because the real Tom Thomson is best known for the 300 or so oil sketches – most of them 8 by 10 inches or even smaller – he made while working and travelling in the vicinity of Algonquin Park, using a portable sketching box. Tom is first shown in profile, looking out at the lake and opposite shore as he paints, and then turning his body so that the painting he holds is almost parallel to the screen, and positioned in the centre of the screen-image. Even when the film is projected on a large scale, this painting is not entirely legible, although it is clearly in the style of Thomson's little sketches, which are admired for their modernist qualities – the bold shapes and strong outlines, the liveliness and quickness of their execution, and their dramatic coloration and expressivity. The camera does not zoom in on this painting, though, and so Wieland ensures that this hand-held rectangle of painted scenery remains visibly inserted into the larger cinematic landscape. The painting becomes an island of stillness, surrounded by panoramic expanses of moving water and air. The camera captures an effect of hazy sunlight, moreover, and the impact of the cinema's immense rectangle of pro-

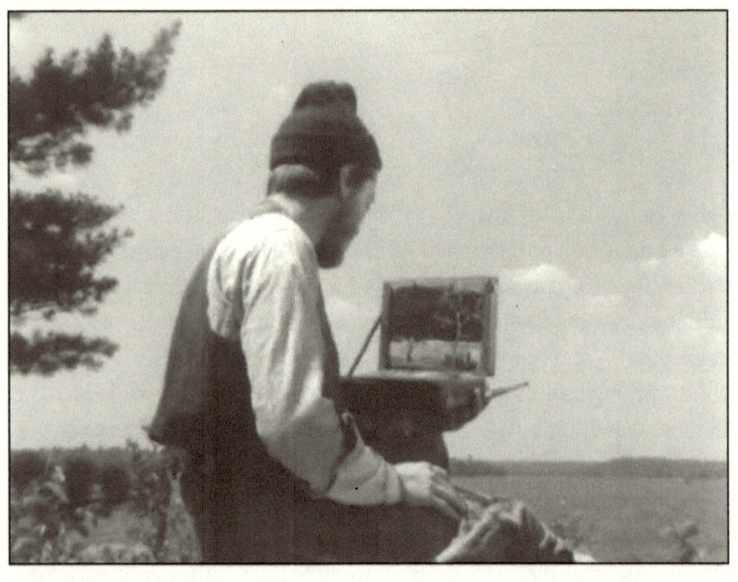

2.1. Tom painting in the 'north country.' Canadian Filmmakers Distribution Centre.

jected light is yet another point of comparison with the opaque surface of the painting.

This scene is important for the explicit contrast it provides between painted and filmed landscape views, but also because it is virtually the only moment in the film when the artist is to be seen on his own within the natural environment, engaged in creative expression. The scene does not last very long; it occurs rather late in the film and is preceded by scenes of urban life, social and romantic negotiation, and psychic unease. This interlude of artistic activity is soon followed by climactic outbursts of anger, lust, and violent death. Nonetheless, it is an important scene, because it exemplifies how the film as a whole reframes Tom Thomson's artwork and the artist's supposedly solitary immersion in nature. The foundational act of *plein-air* painting, for which Thomson and the Group of Seven are famous, is restaged by Wieland, and, indeed, *The Far Shore* complicates the notion that their artwork merely makes nature available for our visual appreciation.

If this scene of Thomson painting outdoors is anomalous in *The Far Shore*, in fact, most of the film takes place not outside in natural settings, but rather within the precincts of the city – mostly within the bourgeois interior spaces associated with Ross and Eulalie. I am nonetheless arguing that landscape plays a hugely important role in the narrative structure and overall meaning of *The Far Shore*. The eventual relocation of the story to the 'north country' is crucial, as this setting serves to make clear that the land has been entwined all along in the destiny of these people. While the main narratological impetus of the film is provided by an obstructed and illicit love affair, the land plays an equally important role within the narrative, as an elusive object of desire for all the main characters. This is so for Tom in his capacity as an artist who is determined to claim this place aesthetically and for Ross and Cluny, who want to possess the territory in material terms. Eulalie, too, in a rather more ambiguous sense, will seek personal fulfilment through this particular natural environment; her situation is made evident when she dives fully clothed into the same lake Tom had previously been painting. All of these competing interests become part of the landscape vision put forward by *The Far Shore*.

Prior to *The Far Shore* Wieland had made two films that addressed the contemporary relevance of Canadian landscape representations: *Rat Life and Diet in North America* (1968) and *Reason Over Passion* (1969). *Rat Life and Diet in North America*, as previously mentioned, was a fable-like story that traced the protagonists' escape from the United States to a lush and fecund destination called Canada. Wieland's *Reason Over Passion*, released in the following year, is quite different, as it is a feature-length film of 80 minutes, consisting of coast-to-coast scenery whizzing by as if the entire country were seen from a moving vehicle, with the non-diegetic addition of voice and electronic beeping sounds. The phrase 'Reason over passion' appears superimposed onto the moving images in endlessly scrambled versions, turning then Prime Minister Pierre Elliott Trudeau's maxim for governance into an absurdity. Wieland's *Reason Over Passion* is a technologized landscape vision, made possible by moving vehicles and mobile viewing machines, and it also features what might be called ideological mechanisms, such as the flag, the national anthem, and the national leader. Thus does Wieland suggest that landscape might be experienced in subjective, embodied (and passionate) terms, but it is inevitably the result of technological and political processes as well. And if *Rat Life and Diet in North America* held out the promise of Canadian landscape as a refuge and place of rest, the unceasing motion of *Reason Over Passion* seems to impede any such respite. There is no moment of stillness, and no possibility of contemplating the landscape from a stable position.

On occasion, Wieland spoke of the three films – *Rat Life and Diet in North America, Reason Over Passion, The Far Shore* – as a trilogy; this is quite illuminating, as what unites these three films, which are otherwise very different in mood and genre affiliation, is their concern with landscape, especially with the imbrication of (Anglo-) Canadian identity and landscape imagery.[1] Wieland also referred to *The Far Shore* as '*Reason Over Passion* with people.'[2] A concrete example of how this is so is evident in an early scene of *The Far Shore* – as the opening credits are still rolling, in fact: Eulalie has just married Ross, has waved good-bye to her family, and is on her way from rural Quebec to Toronto in her husband's chauffeur-driven car. The camera is situated inside the vehicle, framing her as she sits quietly, barely moving, and looking out the window, which itself functions as a frame for the scenery flying by in a visual blur. (This scene is a kind of reversal of the view of Tom painting, where the painted frame-within-a-frame provides an oasis of stillness.) This technologized landscape as seen from a moving vehicle is precisely the kind of footage that makes up *Reason Over Passion*, but what is strikingly different in *The Far Shore* is the presence of Eulalie in the foreground (fig. 2.2). Even this early in the film, the audience has been given clues about her persona, and we are aware that, as she looks out the window, she is also thinking, dreaming, remembering. In other words, the changeable inner life of this character provides a counterpoint to that flickering landscape image. If *The Far Shore* is '*Reason Over Passion* with people,' as Wieland claimed, it is because the ever-moving landscape image eventually will be thoroughly permeated by narrative and melodramatic affect. While Eulalie is initially seen looking passively at the landscape, the story shows her moving beyond mere spectatorship; by the end of the film she will move directly (and passionately) into the landscape. When we consider *The Far Shore* as part of a trilogy of films, in accordance with the filmmaker's comments, it becomes that much clearer how attuned Wieland was to the convergence of landscape and narrative.

This book argues that *The Far Shore* is a both a film about the meaning of landscape, and a work of landscape art. It is important to ask, though,

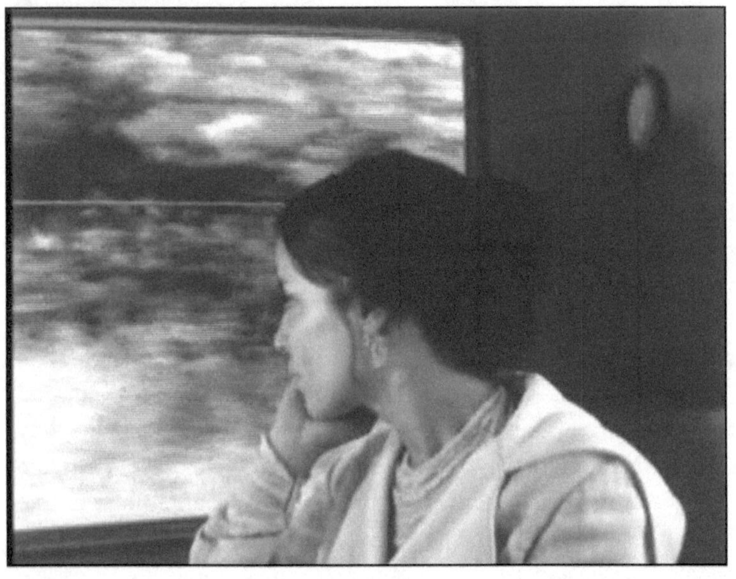

2.2. Eulalie in the car with scenery whizzing by. Canadian Filmmakers Distribution Centre.

how this film differs from other experimental films or mainstream movies that have some kind of natural environment as setting or background. A recent book of essays entitled *Landscape and Film*, edited by Martin Lefebvre, considers some of the ways in which the landscape component of a film (whether mainstream or not) can have a cinematic and aesthetic value, 'that amounts to much more than the mere spatial background that necessarily accompanies the depiction of actions and events.'[3] This raises crucial questions: How can landscape be regarded as something more than background, margin, or supplement to the narrative? How can landscape become something worthy of interest in its own right? Lefebvre's own essay in this book considers the value accorded to cinematic landscape by contrasting 'two modes of spectatorial activity: a narrative mode and a spectacular mode.' In the former case, the landscape component of a film will be seen but barely noticed because the narrative is so strongly asserted, whereas the 'spectacular' mode signals the possibility that the landscape can become a discrete object of contemplation. 'The interruption of the narrative by contemplation has the effect of isolating the object of the gaze, of momentarily freeing it from its narrative function.'[4] I understand this comment to mean that under certain circumstances the cinematic scenery can be provisionally detached from the narrative, and once 'freed' from this dependence, it can stand on its own terms, having become the kind of landscape that is appreciated in aesthetic terms.

Lefebvre admits to borrowing from art-historical discussions in the formulation of his argument, but he seems to rely on a rather conservative art-historical ideal of a pure or autonomous landscape image. The interdisciplinary scholar W.J.T. Mitchell has sharply criticized the tendency (among certain art historians) to describe a 'teleology of landscape' that culminates in a pure, modernist, all-natural image. Mitchell describes this model: 'pure landscape is a painting in which natural scenery is depicted with no adulteration of narrative, allegory, drama, or other textual elements; ideally, in its purest form, pure landscape is even free of any human figures that might suggest an interpretable situation.'[5] But the dominance of the 'pure' landscape is a relatively recent occurrence, and it is possible to tell a rather different story about the development of the landscape genre. In the history of western art there is a very strong tradition of pictures of natural sites and phenomena that are also filled with human figures: this historicized and inhabited version of the landscape genre would include the mythological transactions staged in the seventeenth-century landscape paintings of Nicolas Poussin and the historically specific actions performed by people in the landscapes of the nineteenth-century artist Gustave Courbet. It is this tradition (rather than the pure, autonomous genre of landscape evoked by Lefebvre) that can most persuasively be likened to narrative cinema.

Both Lefebvre and Mitchell's writings are contributions to an ongoing, cross-disciplinary debate about what landscape art can provide, aesthetically and culturally. Does landscape make us aware of the beauty, sublimity, or radical alterity of nature? How important are composition, spatial organization, figure-ground relationships, and all those other pictorial/formal issues? Can painted or cinematic landscapes continue to aestheticize the natural world even while telling complex stories about politics, ecological strife, and personal interaction? The most interesting examples of landscape art and the most compelling examples of scholarship, it seems to me, are those that emphasize the interrelatedness of these questions.[6] In opposition to the notion of an autonomous landscape picture, Wieland's films and artworks attempt to forge an aesthetics of landscape that accommodates such narrative complexity.

Throughout *The Far Shore* there is a sustained tension between narrative and landscape: matters of human interest and history might be positioned in the foreground, but the natural world is always much more than a background to the story; nor does it ever become a pure object of contemplation. Wieland's approach to landscape is indeed announced in the opening scenes of the film. I mentioned earlier that the plot does not contrive to remove the characters from the city until over an hour into the film, but this is not entirely true. There is a fairly lengthy scene before the opening credits roll, which shows Eulalie and Ross in the Quebec countryside, before they marry and begin a life together in Toronto. The film actually does open with all-natural imagery: first, clouds are seen moving across the sky, then the camera slowly descends to show summery treetops blowing in the wind, and still lower, a tranquil riverside scene is revealed. When the main characters move into the frame, however, their first words spoken directly to each other concern the road and bridge that Ross has been contracted to build on this piece of land. That is, the landscape viewed by the protagonists at this moment, an image that is simultaneously made available to the viewing audience, is subject to change and is historically contingent. Eulalie then forestalls Ross's attempt to speak romantically by blurting out that he is being cheated by her brother, who is a lawyer involved with this very building project. They talk about her ex-fiancé, who had broken off their engagement, and Eulalie also mentions her young niece's loneliness living in this place and suggests that she shares this sentiment. Eulalie then wanders off by herself and stands at the water's edge gazing across the expansive space. This striking shot, in its framing, composition, and lighting, is reminiscent of the late nineteenth/early twentieth-century Pictorialist style; here, Wieland introduces what seems to be a rather nostalgic picture of an attractive woman, perfectly complemented by gentle scenery. But Wieland destabilizes the identity of both this particular place (we have just learnt that it is about to be irrevocably transformed) and this particular woman (we already sense the complexity of her inner life, despite the calm smile). Thus, from the opening scene landscape is established in relation to actions, transactions, conversations, gazes, and gestures, all made by characters whose very identity is caught up in that landscape. Another issue that complicates the meaning of landscape in the film relates to its very visibility, because, after the opening scene set in the Quebec countryside, it is the 'north country' that becomes the main object of interest and desire, but the northern Ontario territory in question will be talked about, argued over, and referenced in many different ways before it actually appears on the screen as visual representation.

Thomson on Film

Eulalie appears juxtaposed to specific landscapes at the beginning and end of the *The Far Shore*, but otherwise it is Tom who is consistently associated with and defined by the land, as a maker of landscape pictures and as someone, we are informed, who has greater knowledge and facility in the natural world than any of the other characters. He knows that north country 'like the back of his hand,' as Ross and Cluny angrily remind each other when he refuses to help them find the elusive deposits of silver they want so desperately. Compared with everyone else in the story, it seems that Tom is at home in Canada's natural environment. Before we move on to complicate this question and to further address Wieland's treatment of her fictional landscape painter, it should be noted that Thomson has been re-presented, imaginatively resurrected, and fictionalized in numerous poems, stories, plays, and moving pictures.

Two filmic representations of Thomson preceded Wieland's: *West Wind* (1944) was made by the National Film Board of Canada for the National Gallery of Canada, and *Was Tom Thomson Murdered?* (1969) was a CBC television production. Both films were presented as documentaries, although the genre itself, of course, is no guarantor of truth-value and, in fact, they are quite different kinds of film. *West Wind* was released when Canada was at war, and it is no coincidence that the director of the film, Graham McInnes, was also responsible for a string of military-related films made at the NFB in the mid- to late 1940s. The voice-over narration that accompanies the filmic images announces immediately: 'Deep in the heart of every man lives an image of his land familiar and strong, to arouse and inspire loyalty.' This film was clearly meant to strike a patriotic chord by presenting Thomson as an exemplary Canadian subject and his artwork as the very picture of a beloved and threatened homeland. It is an unusual documentary portrait, though, as no photograph or moving image of Tom Thomson is used. Rather, we are shown various boys and men facing away from the camera or averting their gaze and going about their business of camping, portaging, or paddling; this host of faceless surrogates seem to stand in for the artist. Strangely, the 1969 television production, while more specifically focused on the circumstances of the artist's death, was equally reluctant to put a face to the Thomson icon. As Sherrill Grace comments, 'we only ever see him synecdochically – as a hand on a paddle or brush – or in a soft-focus distant shot ... thus he remains a mystery, a symbolic form.'[7] *West Wind* is also remarkable for its depiction of an entirely male world, without a sister, mother, female lover, friend, or acquaintance appearing even in the background. (It is partly because such an extreme masculinization of Thomson's life and art became naturalized over time that Wieland's introduction of Eulalie into the artist's life story seems so startling.) Thomson's 'passion' for the land and for painting is announced, but overall this is a dispassionate and oddly depersonalized account of creative endeavour. Only the musical score by John Weinzweig manages to suggest melodramatic twists and turns even while nothing of this nature is shown on-screen.

In contrast to these two films, then, *The Far Shore* makes no claims to documentary-style truth; instead, the film initiates a kind of imagined conversation across time between two practising landscape artists:

Wieland herself in the 1970s, and Thomson in the 1910s. Judging by the film itself as well as from comments made by Wieland over the years, she seemed to genuinely admire the paintings made by Thomson and the Group of Seven, even while, as I have suggested, her artworks set out to dislodge this earlier episode of Canadian art from its institutional calcification. But if Wieland did seem to heroize Thomson in some ways, this did not include mimicking his *plein-air* painting practice, by setting up an easel in the woods. She had trained as a painter, and in principle there was nothing to stop her from travelling to Algonquin Park or Bon Echo Park or some comparable location to immerse herself in that natural environment and to then render it in the form of paint on canvas. Wieland instead opted to make landscapes using a range of materials and media, and, most powerfully, it is film (as a visual technology) and cinema (understood as a form of visual narrative) that come up against the tradition of modern landscape painting.

Thomson Mythmaking

Thomson became a 'myth' or an icon of Canadiana inasmuch as his art practice has been institutionalized, alongside the Group of Seven. A visit to the National Gallery of Canada in Ottawa confirms the extent to which 'Canadian Art' is still largely configured around its Group of Seven holdings, as if this were the natural 'ground' or baseline against which all other examples of Canadian art must be measured.[8] Over the years, these paintings have been ubiquitous in reproduced form as well – as posters distributed nationally to schools, on calendars, stamps, government publications, and so on. These landscapes eventually became a kind of visual code for identifying a stable and unified 'Canada,' as if the artworks not only represented wild scenery, but also tapped into some timeless, unchanging wellspring of Canadian identity. It must be noted that the individual members of the Group of Seven were only intermittently committed to a nationalist agenda, and in the case of Thomson, who was not much of a letter writer and left few accounts of his aesthetic ambitions, there is no evidence that he understood his role as artist to be that of nation-builder.

There have been many critics of the myth making surrounding the Group of Seven. The 2007 book *Beyond Wilderness: The Group of Seven, Canadian Identity, and Contemporary Art*, edited by John O'Brian and Peter White, is an important publication in this respect, as it brings together a selection of texts written over the last twenty years or so that expand and complicate the story of Canadian art. It is argued that the transformation of Canada's natural environment into a visually and intellectually stimulating artefact does not occur in a cultural vacuum; the authors in this volume thus bring forward repressed issues of race, gender, land claims, economic imperatives, and so on.[9] In historical terms we are reminded that, at the height of the Thomson/Group fascination with the wild-looking scenery to the north of Toronto, this particular stretch of 'north country' was simultaneously targeted by speculators, businessmen, and mining and logging companies, among others. Whether, as Paul Walton claims, the Group's goals vis-à-vis the Canadian landscape were right in sync with such opportunistic business practices,[10] it is clear that everybody concerned, both artist and entrepreneur, wanted to extract something of value from the land. Such overlapping interests are indeed what Wieland shows us in *The Far Shore*.

To a certain extent, the authors represented in *Beyond Wilderness* are responding to a reactionary discourse that has enveloped Thomson and the Group of Seven, rather than directly challenging the artwork itself. The powerful discourse in question goes beyond writings about art to encompass the many discussions of Canadian literature and cultural production that focus on landscape and includes those geotropic metaphors that have found their way into many an attempt to delineate a national identity. A landscape-related trope that circulated widely around the time of Wieland's film was that of the 'garrison mentality,' put forward by the literary theorist Northrop Frye in the 1960s. The author argued that it is because 'small and isolated communities [are] confronted with a huge, unthinking, menacing, and formidable physical setting' that Canadian writing acquired its paradigmatic narrative structure.[11] Frye was indeed concerned with community, but other authors would further essentialize and de-historicize that moment of contact with nature; thus, Gaile McGregor, writing in 1985, described a 'beleaguered human psyche attempting to preserve its integrity in the face of an alien, encompassing nature.'[12] In such formulations, Canadian culture arises in response to a natural world that is construed as forever 'menacing' and 'alien.' The idea that all Canadians share this underlying fear of nature surely is exaggerated, but there is an important issue here, related to the concept of wilderness. About Thomson's paintings, we can ask whether they represent the natural world as a menacing, alien, threatening force, out to 'beleaguer' his own or other people's psyches, or whether his artwork posits a sense of wonder and respect for the non-human natural world. Is Thomson so fascinating because he is the exception (someone who feels at home in the forest) that proves the rule – that non-Native Canadians feel alienated from the natural environment? And if Thomson did love the wild qualities of nature, is it because he himself was at least partly a wild man? We seem to have come full circle, asking once more: why did a modern, increasingly urban and industrialized nation-state become so obsessed with wilderness imagery?

The intellectual groundwork for Tom Thomson's less-than-civilized persona was laid by the 1925 book *A Canadian Art Movement: The Story of the Group of Seven*, written by Fred Housser. The author says that 'the heart of the bush ... was the only place Thomson felt at home' and that 'the cries of the wild were in every stroke of his brush'; he also claims that Thomson 'was untrained as a painter. His master was Nature.'[13] The idea that Thomson was untrained as an artist is ridiculous, of course; it is a matter of historical record that he worked for many years as an engraver, designer, and commercial illustrator, while his fraternization with the other Group artists gave him access to the world of modernist European art. In a more measured account, the art historian Denis Reid describes how Thomson struggled with the legacy of Post-Impressionism to forge his own style, helped along by A.Y. Jackson in particular.[14] In any case, landscape painting is a venerable cultural artefact whose codes and conventions have been transmitted from artist to artist over many hundreds of years. It is useful to remember that the two-dimensional, illusionistic landscape picture did not exist in North America until the Europeans brought the art form over, along with all their other cultural and artistic baggage. Nonetheless, a glance at the Internet reveals the persistence of the story about Thomson being a self-taught, untrained artist who wandered into the woods one day and picked up a paintbrush.

Housser insists, though, that Thomson and the Group were examples of 'a new type of artist; one who divests himself of the velvet coat and flowing tie of his caste, puts on the outfit of the bushwacker and prospector.'[15] Somewhat ironically, this statement is also an admission that the artists were playing dress-up: they had to don the appropriate costumes and act the part of people who really belong in the woods and mountains. Housser's comments about changes of costume are amusing, but also are relevant to this discussion because in some respects *The Far Shore* is a 'costume drama' movie, and as such it reintroduces the 'velvet coat and flowing tie' into the story of Canadian art, as one of the socio-stylistic components that goes into the making of a national landscape vision. In Wieland's film, behaviour and apparel change as characters move between the city and the country, and this multiplicity of personas and clothing itself is an important part of the story. In one scene in the film Tom is seen to be on very friendly terms with a family of working people in the countryside; he shares a meal, fiddle music, and dancing in their simply furnished home. But the woman he has fallen in love with, and who also happens to be the character in the film who is most appreciative of his art, is a sophisticated, Debussy-playing, elegantly dressed woman (fig. 2.3). It should also be noted that while the historical figure of Tom Thomson might have resembled a 'bushwacker' on occasion, other sources have claimed that 'there was a streak of the dandy in him too, and he affected flamboyant silk shirts.'[16] *The Far Shore* provides some insight, then, into how a painter of landscapes must negotiate the solitude of *plein-air* activity on the one hand, and the ambitions, commercial interests, and social interaction of the city on the other. So, too, do the paintings themselves inevitably move into and through social space; those artworks the *plein-air* artist created in solitude, in some remote place, will end up back in Toronto or Paris or another metropolitan centre, having assumed an identity as cultural artefacts – to be shown, talked about, bought, and sold.

In no sense does Wieland's film set out merely to debunk Tom Thomson, but it could certainly be claimed that Thomson appears as both a deconstructed and a reconstructed hero. The history and meaning of Canadian landscape art was not taken for granted by Joyce Wieland. So *The Far Shore*, insofar as it is an alternative telling of Thomson's life and death, is a kind of art-historical revisionism. Wieland comes across as a great admirer of the art itself, but not of the conservative discourse that, fifty years after Thomson's death, had come to surround both the man and his art. She reinterprets the figure of Thomson – and, by extension, the whole Group of Seven phenomenon – as much more than an exercise in personal expressivity: a story of male camaraderie and an emblem of nationalist well-being. However, Wieland does not dispute the allure of remote and wild places or the artist's vision of a distant far shore; I would even say she reinstates the mysterious fascination with the wildness of nature, as a legitimate desire, that acknowledges the

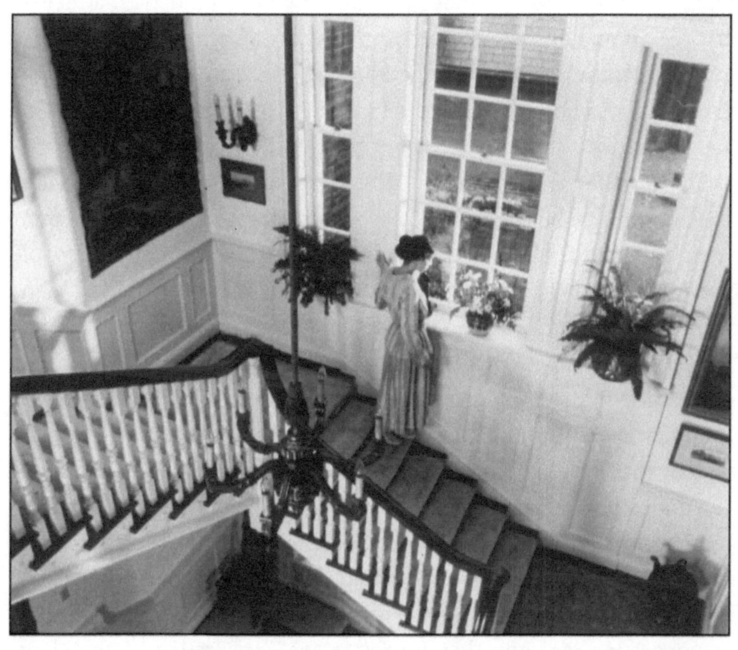

2.3. Eulalie looking out the window of the Rosedale mansion. National Gallery of Canada, Library and Archives, Ottawa.

limits of human control and of our symbolic systems. Writing about the death of Thomson, Housser suggests that 'only a few of those who read of the tragedy in the newspapers would appreciate what the loss of a comparatively obscure painter meant in the imaginative life of the country.'[17] Wieland's film does not challenge the fundamental belief that the art and life of Tom Thomson can play a key role in 'the imaginative life of the country,' but the story she tells is an alternative way of thinking about how one individual's artwork becomes so important in the creation of a nation's shared imaginative life.

The Far Shore does emphasize that an artist's aesthetic approach to the land cannot be considered in isolation, because at any given moment the land is the object of overlapping interests and desires, of concurrent landscape 'visions.' During the opening courtship scenes in rural Quebec, Eulalie expresses some mild regret that Ross's roads and bridges will change a beloved place, but at this moment such interventions appear to be an inevitable aspect of modernization. Once the plot relocates to Toronto, however, the stakes become greater, and it is evident that Ross envisions a more grandiose kind of territorial expansion and exploitation. We are shown Ross on the premises of his engineering firm, making a confidence-building speech to the assembled staff (fig. 2.4). He tells them that despite the recent recession, which he says is inevitable in a post-war situation, they should not doubt the potential for prosperity that resides in the exploitation of the land: 'There are wonderful opportunities here ... In the north country, there are natural resources, raw materials that can make this land into one of the most powerful nations in the world.' Here Ross functions as a kind of mouthpiece for the consolidated interests of scientific knowledge and expertise and commercial enterprise, while he is overtly part of a greater project of nation-building; Canada now has a chance to become 'one of the most powerful nations in the world,' he proclaims. Immediately after this scene Ross asks Eulalie what she thought of his

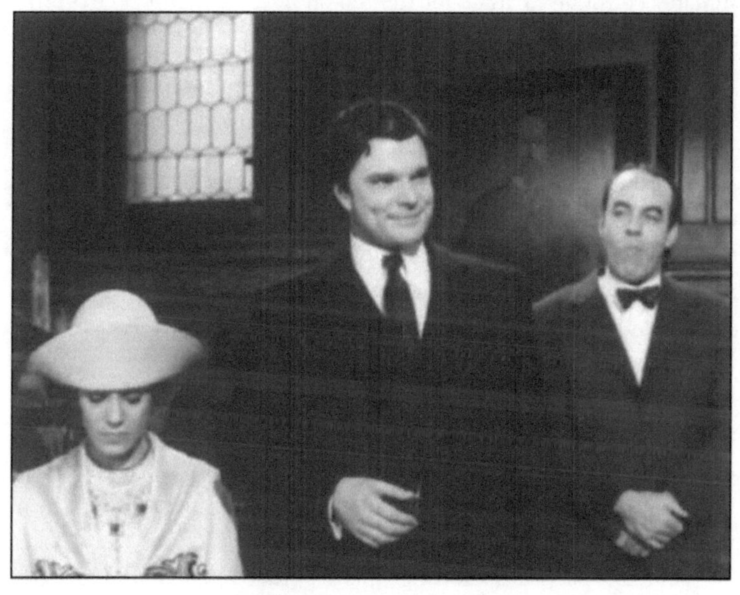

2.4. Ross's nation-building speech to his employees. Canadian Filmmakers Distribution Centre.

speech (she jokes that some people were yawning, and he is offended), and somewhat later he announces to her that he wants to enter politics and run for Parliament. It is thus apparent that his speechifying will continue, and whether he is an entrepreneur or an MP, he will presumably continue to argue for the full-on development of the 'north country.'

Desire for Landscape

As mentioned earlier, the land in question is described and argued over a great deal before it is actually shown on-screen. The initial confrontation between Ross and Tom regarding the land takes place in the city; more specifically, after Ross's car has broken down returning from a seasonal winter party, the venue is Tom's shack, where Ross, Eulalie, and Cluny take temporary shelter. Tom is getting wood for the fire when Ross follows him outside to ask if he plans to go north next year, and when he says yes, Ross proposes that Tom work as a guide for 'an exploration team going in to look over my land.' Tom says 'no thanks ... I don't guide for exploration teams,' and when Ross persists, he curtly responds, 'Get someone else.'

While this particular exchange, highlighting Tom's refusal to serve as a guide for Ross's silver-exploration party, was invented by Wieland, there is nothing about Ross's request that contravenes the historical evidence. The real Tom Thomson did not merely enter Alonquin Park as a collector of visual impressions; rather, he worked there as a guide, ranger, and firefighter at various times, alongside other people engaged in many sorts of labour and commerce. Thomson's painting activity was enmeshed with these other activities and with the workaday exploitation of nature. A.Y. Jackson also went on artistic excursions into Algonquin Park, and his later description of the territory and Thomson's relationship to it is striking: 'It was a ragged country; a lumber company had slashed it up, and fire had run through it ... Thomson was much indebted to the lumber companies. They had built dams and log chutes, and had made clearings for camps. But for them the landscape would have been just bush, difficult to travel in and with nothing to paint.'[18] So we learn that the park was no untouched wilderness after all, but it is still astonishing to encounter Jackson's matter-of-fact remark that Thomson was 'indebted to the lumber companies' and his claim that Thomson would have had 'nothing to paint' if it were not for these industrial incursions into the natural environment. This assertion also accords with Walton's more recent description of Thomson country as 'the devastated site of the second great industry to be established, after the fur trade, in the North.'[19]

John O'Brian asks, 'Why, until recently, did industrialized Canadian landscape paintings by the Group of Seven and others, of which there are a sizable number, not also become part of the national imaginary, part of the dominant iconography of nationhood?'[20] To some extent, though, we have been looking at industrialized landscapes all along, and at times the titles and subject matter of many of Thomson's small sketches speak directly to this awareness: *Timber Chute, Burnt Land, Burnt Country, Lumber Camp,* and *Lumber Dam,* among others, attest to the churned up, half-destroyed and half-regenerated environment that Thomson was drawn to. Then we discover that even those dramatically open vistas appearing through a scrim of trees are very often the result of human intervention – but again, this intersection of art and industry has generally been disavowed. This is not to say that Thomson was not fascinated by the elemental forces of nature and the alterity of the non-human, natural world. But this interest never told the whole story, nor does it suffice as a master-narrative for his career as an artist.

In the scene in Tom's shack described above, the argument continues as Ross doggedly tries to persuade Tom to help him, and at this point the other two characters get involved as well.

TOM (*turning to Eulalie*): Have you ever seen land that's been mined for silver?

ROSS: I never said silver.

TOM: It looks like the Western Front after four years of war.

CLUNY: How would a goddam pacifist know a thing like that, eh?

TOM: An old soldier told me.

Both Ross and Tom get angry and raise their voices; Ross goes on to mock Tom's concern for the land and the animals on it, and Tom responds by describing the extent of damage caused by silver mining.

TOM: You find silver there and the rush is on again. They'll be digging that land up clear up to Lake Abitibi.

ROSS: You sound pretty sure it's there.

TOM: Oh, every little bush and rock like the back of my hand.

CLUNY: Son of a bitch ... knows exactly where it is.

ROSS: Is that right, Tom?

TOM: Ross, you're rich enough; leave the land alone.

The scene turns into one of physical confrontation when Cluny furiously flings the bottle he is drinking from across the room, at which point Tom tussles with Cluny and throws him outside, which then becomes the pretext for Ross to start physically attacking Tom as well.

If we know that the historical figure of Thomson was acutely aware of occupying and painting a 'devastated site,' Wieland's film puts the fictional Tom in a position where he has an opportunity to take a stance on one specific instance of northern development. And it is possible to regard this struggle over a relatively small piece of land as a symptom of the larger, ongoing debate about the Canadian territory – who owns it, who makes decisions about it, who profits from it ... and what kind of environmental, social, or psychic damage might occur when stewardship of the land is in the wrong hands. Certainly these are the issues that preoccupied Wieland as she was making this film in the early 1970s. The 'development' of Canada's northern lands was in the news more than ever throughout this period, and the most controversial project was the monumental hydroelectric power system undertaken on the east coast of James Bay in northern Quebec. This endeavour involved the diversion of three rivers and the flooding of 11,500 square kilometres of land (as is often noted, an area the size of New York state) that was home to Cree and Inuit peoples. During the 1970s the Cree actively campaigned against the James Bay Project, and decried the government's exclusion of First Nations people from the decision-making process. Philip Awashish, one of the young Cree leaders who emerged to galvanize this protest, announced this bitter truth on many occasions: 'The region has been utilized almost exclusively by the Cree people who have no voice in the decision-making body which [is now] planning the development of resources in the area.'[21] While the film was taking shape, Wieland participated in demonstrations and fund-raising activities with the Cree.

By the time Wieland came to make *The Far Shore,* therefore, she regarded the north as a politically contested and ecologically threatened environment, and this belief was evident in both her activist commitments and her artwork. One of her quilted artworks shown in the 1971 True Patriot Love exhibition, *Water Quilt,* is a blatantly politicized piece of landscape art: the delicately embroidered Arctic flowers on the quilt-like object could be lifted up to reveal excerpts from a book by James Laxer, criticizing Canadian government plans to sell 'bulk water' to the United States. So, as Wieland set out to make landscape art in the 1960s and 1970s, water and electrical power were the key resources determining the meaning and appearance of the land, just as the lumber and mining industries had been in Thomson's time. In both cases these industrial/commercial incursions impact directly on the artist's attempt to aesthetically transform the natural environment and to produce an artistic landscape image for the Canadian public. In this sense Wieland's period-piece film provided a historical context for contemporary debates about the development of the 'north country,' whether this was understood as an area proximate to Toronto or, in more general terms, as the vast territory north of the forty-ninth parallel.

When Tom is first introduced to Eulalie (and to the viewer), it is in that same rustic shack where the fight later breaks out. In the earlier scene, Ross and Eulalie have dropped by, and it seems at that juncture that Ross's relation to Tom is something between a friend and a patron. Entering the shack, Ross glances quickly at the painting installed on large easel (a painting that much resembles Tom Thomson's *The West Wind*) and immediately announces that he wants to buy it, at which point Tom (good-humouredly, as all the players in the story are quite friendly at this point) suggests that he'd prefer to finish the painting first. Later, Ross will try to get a Toronto art dealer interested in representing Tom, but he is shocked to hear from him that Tom's paintings are a bad investment, and then he acts as if he had been tricked into supporting Tom's career. With these episodes a wedge is driven between such artworks and the merchant/entrepreneurial class, who were, historically speaking, destined to become the patrons of Canada's modern school of landscape painting. Toronto businessmen along the lines of *The Far Shore*'s Ross character would indeed be crucial players in this story that culminates in the cultural enthronement of Thomson and the Group of Seven. It is partly because Ross's interest in owning Tom's paintings is interrupted that Wieland can tell a different story, one in which this type of landscape art is not positioned as the exact counterpart of that gung-ho entrepreneurial ambition to achieve mastery over the Canadian territory.

In 1974, just as Wieland was developing her alternative-history script, Barry Lord was bringing an explicitly leftist analysis to Canadian art history: 'Landscape historically is a bourgeois art form. To achieve a national art of the Canadian landscape, therefore, the support of a national bourgeoisie was needed.'[22] Lord is not unsympathetic to Tom Thomson, but he describes Thomson and the Group of Seven painters as bound to the aspirations and economic imperatives of their bourgeois patrons. Wieland's fiction about a troubled relationship between artist and patron suggests something rather different: while the film does reveal behind-the-scenes workings of class values and economic interest, the figures of Tom and Eulalie provide a more emancipatory desire for landscape, which cannot so easily be appropriated by the dominant class. In Wieland's retelling, the art is powerful, and as such it is not condemned to remain forever institutionally compromised and ideologically boxed in.

Subsequent to the clash between Ross and Tom, the characters' relationship to the land becomes even more complicated, owing to the increased agency of Eulalie. At the time of the altercation over silver mining, she is off to one side in the shack, and although she shouts at the men to stop fighting, she is still peripheral to the argument under way. In the next scene, however, Eulalie is wishing her husband well as he sets off to an important business meeting, while she then sets off on her own to Tom's shack, ostensibly to apologize on Ross's behalf. But in effect, the argument over the value of the land marks a turning point for her as well, as she begins to shift her allegiance, as well as her libidinal and imaginative energy, to Tom.

During the winter months of 1915–16 and 1916–17 the historical Tom Thomson occupied a shack in Toronto that was refurbished for him by his rich friends – his fellow painter, the independently wealthy Lawren Harris, and Doctor MacCallum, the devoted supporter and collector of this school of landscape painting – when Thomson could no longer afford to rent space in the so-called Studio Building. This wooden structure, originally adjacent to the Studio Building in Toronto's Rosedale

Ravine, itself would become a cult object; it was eventually bought and relocated by the McMichael Collection, and today it is set in a pleasant garden in Kleinburg, Ontario, where visitors can peer inside and imagine the genius at work. For the film, Wieland had a facsimile of this shack constructed, for which Ann Pritchard created an interior decor according to written and visual accounts of Thomson's occupancy; this resurrected shack was then reintroduced into the Toronto ravine. Yet in *The Far Shore* the shack occupied by Thomson functions as more than a studio, as it serves as an important site of encounter for all the characters in the film. The shack is situated in an ambiguous zone, moreover – in the middle of the city, but also in the forest-like ravine. After Eulalie's initial visit to Tom, a beautiful sequence shows Eulalie as she leaves her mansion home: the camera follows her as she walks down a long, winding path into the wooded area that leads to Tom's shack; with this descent into the ravine her escape is already halfway accomplished.

What then follows is a sequence of short scenes inside the shack, showing Eulalie visiting, talking to Tom as he paints (fig. 2.5), and sharing a meal he has cooked; we also see them singing and playing music together. Throughout, they are comfortably ensconced in the confined space of Tom's studio home. These scenes of two people getting to know each other and falling in love are very naturalistically rendered and at the same time carefully choreographed, as the actors' harmonious gestures and poses make it evident that an intimate bond has formed between them, even though they are not shown touching each other. However, the last of the shack scenes breaks this spell: the lovers sit close together, with arms draped around chairs and their hands almost touching, as Eulalie attempts to elicit a more direct avowal from Tom. At this point the interaction and conversation between them echoes the earlier confrontation between Tom and Ross. Just as her husband had suggestively asked Tom, 'Going up north next year?'

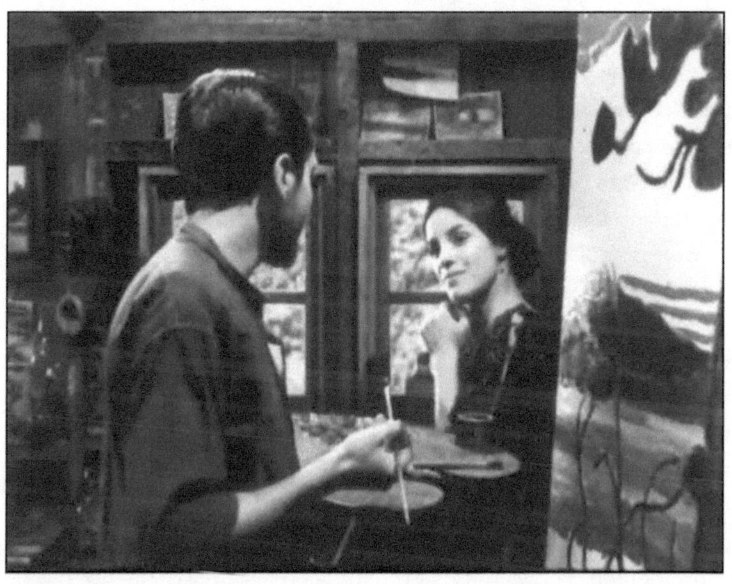

2.5. Eulalie visiting Tom in his shack as he paints. Canadian Filmmakers Distribution Centre.

while wanting something from the artist, so too will Eulalie have an ulterior motive when she questions him about his plans to leave the city. Their conversation is halting and awkward:

EULALIE: When will you be back?
TOM: I don't know.
EULALIE: ... You will come back?
TOM: Not here ... I won't try to paint here again.
EULALIE: Ross said that I was to remember you ... that people will ask me ... What shall I tell them? (*He does not respond*)
EULALIE (*heatedly*): I'll tell them that you were in love with a rock, and a tree, and a piece of sky.

She rises up and begins to gather her coat, but he still does not reply, and the camera stays on his rather stony, expressionless face as she exits on the right, until there is a shot of her departing silhouette through the window of the shack. These angry words that Eulalie hurls at Tom, this accusation that he is only 'in love with a rock,' is what profoundly complicates what might otherwise be understood as an either/or approach to the land. The film initially suggests a contrast, and a confrontation, between Ross's profit-making entrepreneurial projects and Tom's aesthetic sensitivity to the natural world. Wieland seems to be on Tom's side in this respect, and yet Eulalie's intrusion into the story of his life and art suggests that something crucial was still missing from this aesthetic interaction with nature. Eulalie's words can be read as an indictment of the 'pure landscape' concept – the idea that the visual appreciation of nature can be detached from other aspects of life. Thomson's 'love' for rocks, trees, and skies is surely necessary for a landscape artist, but Eulalie challenges Tom to include human, erotic love in his passion for the (natural) world. What is the value of a picture that shows a rock, a tree, and a piece of sky? *The Far Shore* asks us to reconsider this rather fundamental question and, in the process, puts into question what the art of Tom Thomson has meant for Canadian art and culture.

If we now return to *The Far Shore*'s abbreviated depiction of Tom engaged in *plein-air* landscape painting, it becomes clear that Wieland was intent on showing how the artist's approach to the land is permeated by both social contracts and personal relationships. At this point in the film the audience views the artist at work, knowing of Eulalie's presence right across the lake, although Tom has yet to become aware of it. Eulalie has accompanied her husband on an outing that is a bizarre combination of mining expedition and rural holiday. Having relocated to this new environment, though, she will finally make a decision about her life. (Chapter 3 will address the circumstances that lead up to this moment.)

The latter section of the film is clearly demarcated as something separate, as Wieland interrupts the naturalism of the filmic action with the dramatic use of an iris shot. The first part of the film closes with a shot of Eulalie lying disconsolate in her darkened bedroom; this picture shrinks to become a circular frame around her face (fig. 2.6), onto which is superimposed the image of a man in a canoe, which gradually becomes brighter and opens up to again fill the screen. From this point on the protagonists are visibly inserted into this 'north country' that until then we have only been hearing about, and it is also from this point that the pace of the film accelerates. Leaving the city behind is by no means an opportunity for a restful change from city life or an escape from daily concerns; instead, the natural environment seems to act as a catalyst, bringing conflicts to the surface.

The latter part of the film follows a group of people as they leave the city and travel to the periphery of socialized space. It is quite evident that the 'natural environment' they find themselves in is not an untouched wilderness, but rather a site of industry (logging and mining)

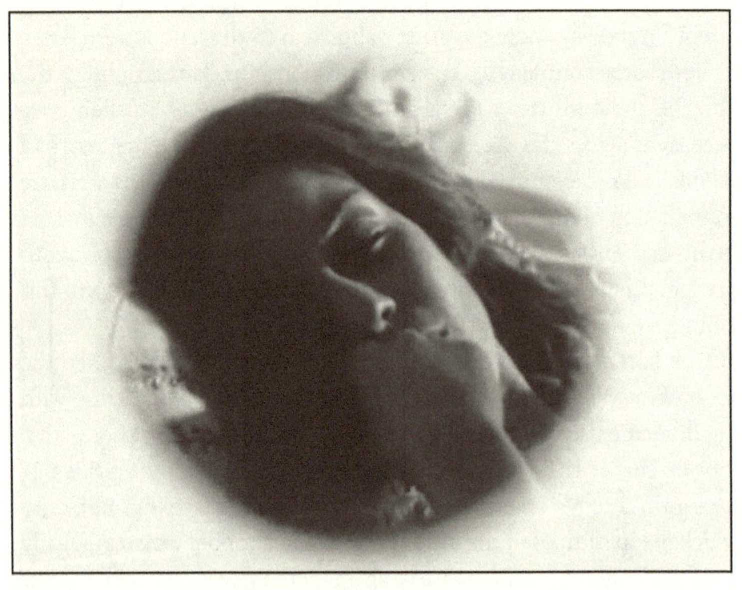

2.6. Iris-shot of Eulalie lying in bed, disconsolate. Canadian Film-makers Distribution Centre.

and tourism; the uniformed maidservant in the lodge where Ross and his party are staying makes it clear that they are certainly not roughing it in the bush. That this is an inhabited place has already been established by the presence of a working-class family, who are Tom's friends from previous visits to the region. Nonetheless, something of importance can happen at this threshold – which is not a full-on wilderness, but is still a site where the natural world is encountered, a site where people are provisionally separated from the usual cultural artefacts and ideological configurations that organize their behaviour. It is here, in this nature/culture between-zone that the characters will undergo a significant transformation. This is how Wieland's landscape vision is different from Thomson's: *The Far Shore* explicitly narrativizes that dialectical tension, between a profound desire for the wildness of nature and, on the other hand, the social bonds, collective aspirations, and intersubjective desires that usually come together in modern cities. If, after his death, Thomson's paintings would be institutionally and ideologically positioned so that they seem to be traces of one man's solitary encounter with nature, going back to this moment before the artist dies becomes a way to expand the meaning of those well-known landscape images. W.J.T. Mitchell's comments about the ostensibly pure landscape genre can be returned to once more, as the author explicitly addresses the relationship between landscape and history: 'What, we might ask, if landscape were to be thought of, not so much as a representation of a "memorable" scene in nature, but as a mechanism for *forgetting* or *erasing* history?'[23] If, for some commentators, the monuments of Canadian art have successfully accomplished the erasure of history, what Wieland instead proposed with *The Far Shore* was to reinsert Thomson's landscapes into a dynamic historical picture.

In the final section of the film, landscape and narrative are completely entwined; there is no possibility that the landscape can be regarded as a discrete object of contemplation, as mere background, or as some kind of decorative addendum to the dramatic content. In the early part of the film, the land in question is talked about repeatedly, and we encounter it visually only insofar as this same territory appears as aestheticized representation in Tom's painting. By the end of the film, these distanced and mediated viewpoints are replaced with a *plein-air* immediacy that can be compared to Thomson's own painting practice. Every character is put to the test, and they confront each other surrounded by the non-human natural world. The contact with nature has the capacity to challenge conventional ways of thought and perception. What nature does, in all of its changeability and wildness and elemental power, is to provide an imaginative counter-force to that which is known and understood.

After a series of dramatic exchanges Eulalie dives into the lake, swimming across a wide expanse of water to reach Tom. This is one of the film's most striking images, as the heroine, conventionally dressed in a long and voluminous skirt, boldly yet gracefully executes her dive off the end of the pier. Wieland herself said about Eulalie's momentous dive into the lake: 'To me this was the most important shot in the film.'[24] She had evidently decided on this significant visual moment early on, and of all the storyboards, sketches, and drawings she created for the making of the film, the largest and most fully finished drawing is that of the Eulalie character suspended in mid-air as she dives, her skirts flowing around her. Wieland presents this dive as a performative gesture; the moment at which she plunges into the lake is the moment when Eulalie leaves her old life behind and claims this landscape for herself. The gesture simultaneously attests to a desire both for Tom and for the landscape. The moment of Eulalie's dive is also a turning point for Tom, as he will shortly join her in the water – no longer in his capacity as detached observer and aestheticizer of nature and not as a labourer in an industrialized forest, but as a lover, fugitive, and murder victim. Wieland thus links the image of Tom painting the landscape

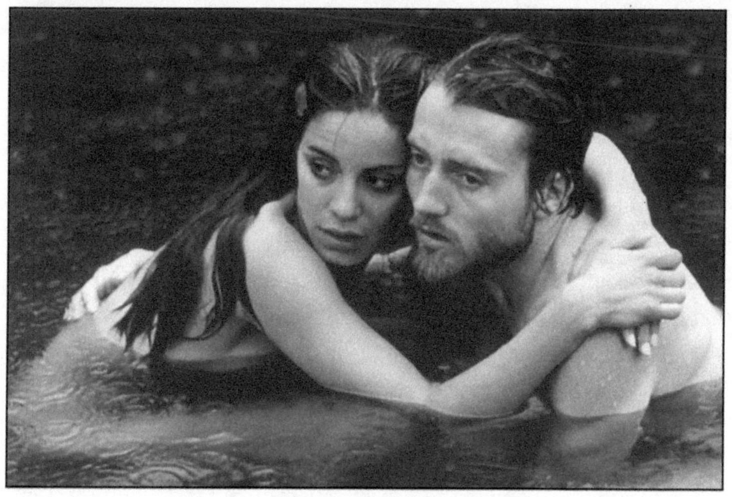

2.7. The lovers in the water, aware that they are being pursued. On-location still photography by Larisa Pavlychenko.

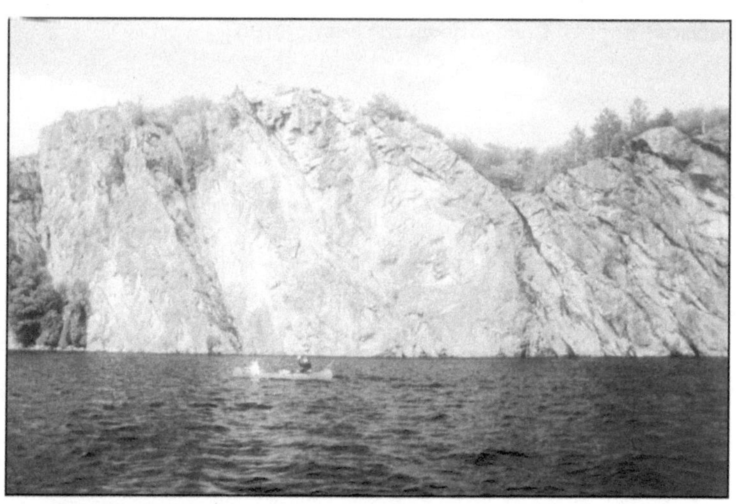

2.8. The lovers attempt to escape, to the 'far shore.' National Gallery of Canada, Library and Archives, Ottawa.

to the image of Eulalie diving into the landscape, as complementary responses to nature.

The last fifteen minutes or so of the film are much more explicitly situated within a 'wild' and unknown natural environment, but this is not presented as an opportunity for the greater visual enjoyment of nature's beauty. There are some short scenes of Tom and Eulalie intimately positioned together in their canoe and in their tent, and there is an extended sequence of making love in the water, but by this point the protagonists are being actively pursued, and indeed, this entire part of the film is characterized by a kind of cinematic paranoia (fig. 2.7). The camera that now provides the viewer with visual access to an expansive and even sublime vision of the natural environment is the same camera that relentlessly follows the lovers around as they try to escape their persecutors (fig. 2.8). Tom and Eulalie know they're being pursued, and we as viewers become complicit with the camera's gaze and with the narrative impulse to track down the errant lovers.

Genre and Gender (Eulalie)

The Far Shore is a profound engagement with the artistic genre of landscape, I have been arguing; envisioning and representing the land is crucial to the film's emplotment, narrative momentum, and character development. Yet, as mentioned, the story does not contrive to move its cast of characters into the natural environment until well over an hour into the film. The story begins with scenes of rural Quebec and ends in Ontario's 'north country,' but between is an urban milieu and, more specifically, a series of Toronto interiors: the Rosedale mansion, Ross's office, a restaurant, Tom's shack. It is the mansion-home of Ross and Eulalie, meanwhile, that provides the most potent conflation of interior architectural space and psychological interiority. Yet this middle part of the film functions at all times in relation to the natural environment – throwing into relief its qualities of exteriority, expansiveness, and wildness. In the Introduction I mentioned a contemporaneous review of *The Far Shore* that critiqued Wieland's apparent inability, or perverse disinclination, to represent the land in all its visual splendour; instead, according to Katherine Gilday, , 'the film-maker grasps the first opportunity to thrust us back into the constraints of interior space.'[1] I suggested that this manoeuvre can be regarded not as a liability, but rather as one of the strengths of the film, because the narrative's inexorable return to the 'constraints of inner space' ensures that we see the landscape only in relation to the concerns and desires of this particular cast of characters. More precisely, it recalls some conventions of melodrama as played out in the history of cinema, whereby interior space is suffused with emotionality and is also the site of social compromise and strained gender relations. *The Far Shore* stages an encounter, as it were, between the art-historical genre of landscape and the filmic genre of melodrama, resulting in a hybrid and cross-disciplinary art form, something that could be described as a melodramatic landscape picture. It is Wieland's introduction of the Eulalie character, moreover, that makes possible this emphasis on gender and genre, ensuring that these questions are joined to the exploration of landscape and nationhood.

In the end, *The Far Shore* does not really disclose the personality and art of Tom Thomson. Wieland's fictional Tom remains elusive – a screen onto which many expectations and desires can be projected. But if it is a commonplace for Canadians to love and admire Thomson, Eulalie now stands in for that desiring Canadian subject, and in Wieland's film it is this invented persona who becomes the primary object of interest. *The Far Shore* tells the story of Eulalie, and it is through her consciousness and gaze that we encounter the Tom character. Thus, the mythic Canadian artist is seen obliquely, seen and desired by a person who is explicitly an outsider, an 'other.' Eulalie's alterity is doubled, in fact, as she is presented as a rather powerless woman in a world ordered by men, and then she is a Québécoise in quasi-exile as the story unfolds in Toronto. There can be no doubt about her outsider status, because early in the film her own husband tells her, without blandishment: 'remember one thing, my dear ... you are the foreigner.' This pronouncement to his wife, made directly after a speech about how Canada is on the verge of becoming a great and powerful nation, also serves to cut her off from the imminent, momentous flowering of nationhood. The bigger question here concerns how someone who is labelled a 'foreigner' can authentically participate in and contribute to Canadian culture. With regard to the story Wieland tells in *The Far Shore* the more immediate concern is whether Eulalie can truly feel at home in her new surroundings, whether she can situate herself in relation to that iconic northern scenery, whether she can become a recognizable figure in the Canadian landscape. These are the lines of questioning posed by *The Far Shore*'s displaced heroine.

The impact of making Eulalie, a woman from Quebec, the central character in a story about Canadian nationhood should not be underestimated. It is important to note that as she was developing the script for *The Far Shore,* Wieland made a short, more experimental film, *Vallières* (1972), about the Québécois militant Pierre Vallières, author of *Nègres blancs d'amérique* (published in French in 1968 and soon thereafter translated into English as *White Niggers of America*), an important intellectual contribution to the French Canadian struggle for a self-determined identity. This is no straightforward documentary portrait by any means, as the film shows only Vallières's mouth as he reads from some of his essays. It was not unusual for left-leaning English Canadians in the 1960s and 1970s to express solidarity with Quebec, and Wieland seemed to genuinely admire the collective coming-to-consciousness that was occurring within the political borders of Canada. Indeed, Wieland's proactive attitude towards nationhood implied that Anglo Canadians needed a wake-up call, that they had to become more self-aware and self-questioning about their national identity – in other words, more like French Canadians in their quest to achieve a newly defined nation of emancipated Québécois. Nor is it coincidental that Vallières distinguished himself among this generation of revolutionaries through his insistence that a feminist transformation must occur alongside, and be interwoven with, the struggle for national self-determination.[2] The character of Eulalie, appearing as an outsider or 'foreigner' at the very heart of Canadian art and culture, is inflected with these contemporary (1970s) concerns. As a woman and as a Québécoise, Eulalie represents part of the struggle, or set of interrelated struggles, over identity and imagination and over the land.

Wieland nevertheless shows that in many ways Eulalie does fit in perfectly with Ross's Toronto home and social world. She is beautiful and elegant and, as such, a suitable 'trophy wife' for Ross. She comes from an elite background (we are shown the wedding party driving away from her brother's impressive-looking house in Chicoutimi), and she has evidently studied the piano seriously enough to consider a career as a concert pianist. She favours the music of the French composer Claude Debussy, and the 'En bateau' and 'First arabesque' pieces that she plays repeatedly serve as a musical motif throughout the film. These are the traits of a cultured, bourgeois individual. Eulalie's life in Toronto is one of tremendous privilege, furthermore: she is waited on by servants and we repeatedly see her clothed in fashionable dresses and opulent furs.

Eventually, though, the film asks us to recognize that Eulalie has an excess of imaginative and libidinal energy, which can no longer be contained within this bourgeois milieu. She reaches a point when she can no longer abide by the 'civilized' state of things – more specifically, the bonds of marriage, her husband's authority, and those rules of social propriety that are meant to determine her behaviour and position in society. So she will attempt to break out of this situation, with and through the personage of Tom. She is the active party in their relationship: she pursues him. While it seems evident that she is attracted to Tom himself, *The Far Shore* makes it clear that Eulalie also yearns to be a committed artist: at home with Ross she tells him of her dream of becoming a concert pianist, but he brushes away this idea as if it were a joke. On another occasion, when the couple is shown having a tête-à-tête dinner in an opulent restaurant, she confides that her strong attachment to music is linked to an episode of temporary childhood deafness, and after recounting this story she directly asks him, 'do you understand?' But Ross is quite evidently unable to empathize with his wife and does not respond directly to the question; he immediately changes the subject to discuss his own political aspirations: 'there's a by-election coming up, the party wants me to run.' When Eulalie finally dives into the lake, when she, too, seeks to immerse herself in the 'north country,' her romantic desire to be with Tom is conjoined with these other unfulfilled desires.

Wieland presents her protagonist Eulalie as a compelling but flawed character. She made a bad decision in marrying Ross and, when we encounter her, she has not been successful at carving out a space for herself in the world. Rather, she is a complex character beset by uncertainty, doubt, moodiness, and melancholy about who she is and what she wants. It is precisely this degree of complexity, and the depth of Eulalie's dissatisfaction, that links this specific heroine invented by Joyce Wieland in the 1970s to a larger feminist project, intent on realigning the gendered terms of filmmaking and artmaking. If Eulalie can be regarded as a feminist prototype, it is because the film's narrative is constructed in accordance with her subjective position and, more specifically, because the dynamic psycho-affective force emanating from this character seems to put pressure on the patriarchal structures that dominate and enclose her, until they begin to fracture. By the time Wieland came to make her film, both first-wave and second-wave feminists had analysed the ways that bourgeois institutions and mores (including patterns of sexual behaviour) functioned to oppress women; also, feminist authors and artists were responsible for envisioning how these same institutions might be transformed.

As it turns out, the period setting of the film is rather interesting with regard to the changing social status of women in Canada. In 1918 Canadian women acquired the right to vote after a long struggle, while in 1919, the year in which the film is set, the right to stand for election to the House of Commons was extended to women across Canada. We learn early on that Eulalie's ex-fiancé is destined for an illustrious career in politics and then that Ross also intends to run for office, but Eulalie, in comparison, is still very far from being such a politically empowered citizen. (Ross goes so far as to describe to Eulalie his fantasy of himself holding forth on one side of the House, with her ex-fiancé [his rival] on the other side and Eulalie looking on from the visitor's gallery.) The story Wieland tells nonetheless brings the story of women's emancipation – the uneven process of women becoming active, desiring, socially integrated subjects – into the history of modern art in Canada. In a sense, the three main characters embody different aspects of modernity. The engineer, Ross, represents the science, technology, and technocratic expertise that create the material foundations of modern life. Tom represents the artistic side of the modernist imagination: from a twenty-first-century perspective we are apt to forget that Thomson and his friends were assertively modern artists and were regarded as such at the time they began exhibiting their work. One critic writing in 1921 described the typical Group of Seven landscape picture as conveying only 'jazzy and momentary sensation,'[3] and while this comment is meant to be derogatory, of course, it does suggest how these artworks succeeded in describing aspects of modern, urban experience, even as the ostensible subject matter of the paintings is remote natural scenery. Then, the proto-feminist figure of Eulalie also bespeaks an important kind of modern transformation. Her quest for self-realization is actually part of a collectively wrought challenge to the political status quo; she is participating in one of the utopian social movements that characterize the modern age.

The second-wave feminism that Wieland participated in was intent on achieving equity throughout the social formation, which meant that private life was to be regarded as a legitimate sphere of political activity and agency. 'Consciousness-raising' groups of women tried to forge a new way of regarding sexuality, relationships with husbands and lovers, family dynamics, and so on, which would be in keeping with a truly comprehensive 'feminist revolution.' *The Far Shore*'s analysis of domestic life and gender roles and its delineation of one woman's attempt to take charge of her own destiny would have resonated for audiences in 1976. The recent exhibition *Wack: Art and the Feminist Revolution* (2007) is a timely assessment of the radical artistic projects of the 1960s and 1970s, and it makes it evident just how much feminist-inflected artists of the time shared Wieland's concerns. A Canadian and Québécois version of this art-historical endeavour has not yet been attempted, but Wieland's work would certainly be of central importance to such a project. *The Far Shore,* insofar as it was an extension of her art practice, should therefore be considered part of this wave of feminist visual art.

The intersection of feminism and film has its own more specialized history, of course, and many aspects of feminist film theory remain relevant for this interpretation of *The Far Shore*. The problem of how to convey a woman's point of view in cinematic terms was much debated in the 1970s, both in relation to the agency of a woman director/narrator, and in speculations about a new kind of feminized gaze. Laura Mulvey's scholarship was crucial in this respect, in establishing a vocabulary to describe the gendered bias of the cinematic apparatus as it follows characters around to tell a story. The camera observes, frames, interprets, and sets in place mechanisms of desire that involve both the characters appearing on screen and the spectators of the film. It was masculine desire and agency that had historically informed the cinematic project, and the gender realignment of cinema would not be easily accomplished, precisely because certain modes of psychic identification were so deeply embedded and because the conventionality of genre often served to reinforce gender roles. The question that preoccupied early feminist filmmakers and theorists alike was whether it was possible to seize hold of and transform this narratological/psycho-sexual machine; Mulvey wrote that an 'alternative cinema must start specifically by reacting against these obsessions and assumptions.'[4] How might cinema be reinvented, so that it better corresponded to feminine desire?

Some film scholars of the 1970s and 1980s critically re-examined those Hollywood movies characterized as 'women's pictures' or 'family melodramas' – referring to emotionally overwrought productions that featured women at the affective epicentre of the story's *Sturm und Drang*. Some instances of the melodrama genre were regarded as a form of social critique, because they seemed to expose the ideological contradictions embedded in the bourgeois family.[5] Feminist scholars also noted, however, the limitations (politically speaking) of this genre. E. Ann Kaplan writes: 'the family melodrama, as a genre geared specifically to women, functions both to expose the constraints and limitations that the capitalist nuclear family imposes on women and, at the same time, to "educate" women to accept those constraints as "natural," inevitable – as "given."'[6] This suggests the complexity of melodrama: it has the capacity to lay bare the dissatisfaction of women trapped within repressive social roles, and the audience is asked to bear witness to how a dammed-up excess of emotion, libido, and inchoate yearning can destabilize the heterosexual couple, the family, or a bigger social formation. However, the kind of narrative closure enacted by such films often results in the women characters' apparently being reconciled to their social roles and to their lot in life.

For Lauren Rabinovitz, Wieland's experimentation with melodrama was significant in two respects. First, she remarks that the tragic finale of *The Far Shore* 'effects a rupture in melodramatic closure,' for unlike many films classified as examples of the melodrama genre, in Wieland's film 'the woman does not return to the space within conventional bourgeois boundaries.' In other words, Wieland manages to subvert that ideological resolution and narrative closure that would restore the female protagonist to a socially respectable role. Rabinovitz also makes the point that Wieland appropriated the melodrama genre, only to transform it from within through an experimental-film aesthetic; she speaks of 'a tension between experimental film strategies and traditional film practices.'[7] My own interpretation of *The Far Shore* departs from Rabinovitz's to the extent that I am interested in how the conventional attributes of melodrama, as they developed within cinematic culture, come up against the landscape genre in its art-historical sense. Certainly, the feminist analysis of Hollywood's melodramatic mode sheds light on the Eulalie character. Melodrama at its most effective seems capable of turning the characters inside out, as it were, so that their psychic life becomes cinematically available, and their interior world fuses with the material world they inhabit. (This is why *mise en scène* is so important in melodramas; Douglas Sirk's films are often singled out in this respect, as characters' inner lives are displaced onto the the décor, furnishings, coloration, and lighting.) What is unusual about Wieland's film is that the genre's familiar build-up of repressed emotion occurs within the context of homes and interior spaces, but then the filmmaker orchestrates a breach with this domestic environment, asking us to imagine instead that this surfeit of melodramatic emotion has leaked out into the natural environment, saturating our collective vision of the Canadian landscape. The melodramatic excess is transferred to the landscape genre as epitomized by the paintings of Tom Thomson.

At Home

Ross's mansion and Tom's shack are the film's most significant interior/domestic sites, and Eulalie moves between these two locations. Home space is often described as a feminine realm, but no easy gendering of domestic space is possible in the case of Ross's house, as this space has been thoroughly decorated and organized according to his needs before his new wife arrives on the scene. Eulalie is not asked or expected to create a home, nor is her presence necessary for the running of the household, which is in the hands of competent servants. Her music initially seems to keep her occupied and to provide her with a legitimate activity within the household, but in one telling scene, the housekeeper enters the parlour to inform her that Ross does not want her to play the piano, because the sound of his wife's playing disturbs him at his work. (It is also relevant that in the earliest scene of the film, back in Quebec, Eulalie expresses to Ross her sense of being a dependant in her brother's home.) In this film the male characters are in control of the domestic arrangements. Interestingly, Tom's shack provides yet another non-feminine domestic milieu, with the important difference that Tom very obviously welcomes Eulalie into his miniature home and makes a place for her even while, in physical terms, there is very little available space. We are also shown scenes of him cooking and serving food to Eulalie as she sits at the table. In a rather remarkable sequence, Tom is painting while carrying on a good-humoured and flirtatious conversation with Eulalie. This echoes an earlier scene where Tom stood by Eulalie's side in her husband's lavishly appointed salon, watching and listening attentively to her performance of a Debussy composition.

Eulalie's physical inhabitation of Ross's house and her relationship to its particular object-world is shown in various ways. The morning after her arrival in Toronto she walks around the house, looking at and lightly touching the surface of things. The house is full of fine furnishings, *objets d'art*, and paintings, all of which bodes well, it seems, for someone of her sensibility. Indeed, Wieland presents us with an interior world that has its own aesthetic dimension, characterized by art nouveau patterns and elements of orientalist fantasy, particularly notable in Eulalie's kimono-like dressing-gown. But aside from the piano, which she immediately takes possession of, Eulalie never seems to achieve more than that initial light and superficial contact with the material abundance belonging to her husband; she is not fully or bodily present in this environment. Eventually, this house and its contents become an oppressive force, and after Tom's departure, when his shack no longer provides her with a temporary refuge, she retreats – physically and psychologically – from the household and its concerns. She takes to her bed, and this retrograde and even masochistic response is reminiscent of how wealthy Victorian-era invalids proved unable to face up to the challenge of their lives. One account of melodrama describes 'a closed, hysterical world bursting apart at the seams in which the protagonists, unable to act upon their social environment, suffered severe psychological and emotional symptoms,'[8] and the description does indeed correspond to Eulalie's predicament at this point in the film. It becomes clear that Eulalie would die a slow death were she to spend the rest of her life in Ross's house. This narrativization of a woman trapped in domestic circumstances (although, as stated above, this is not a case of domestic servitude) speaks to both the 1910s and the 1970s. The feminist discourse of the 1960s and 1970s spoke directly of the subservience of women within the 'normal' heterosexual couple and within the social unit of the patriarchal family.

Wieland shows Eulalie's home life as a suffocating and repressive space, but in narrative terms it also serves another purpose. The constraints of this interior domestic space are also what produce a melodramatic excess: emotional upheaval, the eruption of desire, imaginative visions. As Peter Brooks writes, 'melodrama refuses repression or rather, repeatedly strives towards moments where repression is broken through, to the physical and verbal staging of the essential: moments where repressed content returns as recognition.'[9] It can be argued that *The Far Shore* features a number of such breakthrough moments characteristic of the melodrama genre, even if the action or gesture in question can be quite subtle. One such moment occurs before an intimacy between Eulalie and Tom has developed but immediately after Eulalie has had Tom's newly acquired painting (which the artist personally delivered to her during Ross's absence from the house) hung in her bedroom, above the fireplace. It is evening and she sits alone in the plushly decorated room, quietly concentrating on her needlework. She puts down her stitchery and drinks from a cup of tea while looking up at the artwork; then slowly she gets up and walks towards the painting, which is a composition similar to Tom Thomson's famous *West Wind*: a boldly outlined tree in the foreground, a large expanse of water painted with lively, expressionistic brushstrokes, and the darkened silhouette of mountains on the opposite shore. It is not one of his small, quickly executed sketches, but rather a large and carefully wrought piece in which the landscape has been endowed with a strikingly modern geometry. The movement within this shot is slight, as the figure of Eulalie seems to drift weightlessly across the room towards the painting. It is an almost-silent scene as well, with only the faint diegetic sound of the fire crackling. Eulalie stops in front of the painting, reaches up, and slowly touches a branch of Tom's painted tree, and at the very moment when her fingers make contact with the painting, a few plaintive notes of piano music are heard (fig. 3.1). If the act of looking at a painting is not common in the history of film, there is something additionally strange about seeing someone touch a painting, as we have been taught to keep our distance from what are ostensibly visual artefacts. As Eulalie makes contact with Tom's painting, she replicates, in a way, the tactile, expressive gesture that was the artist's as he applied paint to canvas. She also establishes contact with a vivid landscape image, and what Wieland thus conveys is how a work of art can affect a particular individual. With this minimal but telling gesture, and with the accompanying piano sounds that seem to belong to Eulalie's inner life, Wieland does stage a transformative moment in this woman's consciousness, a moment of awakening, when 'repression is broken through.'

Immediately afterwards Eulalie proceeds to throw open the french doors of her bedroom, and she stands looking outside with the wind blowing her hair and dressing-gown – until Ross enters the room, shuts

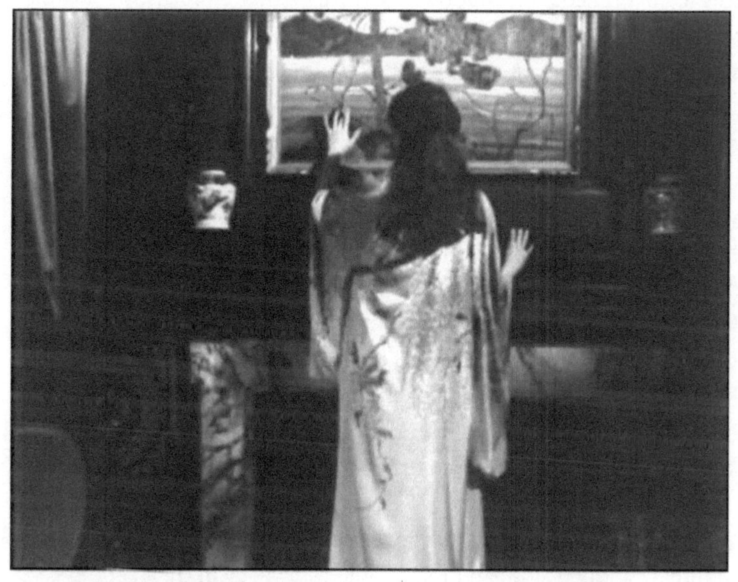

3.1. Eulalie makes contact with Tom's painting. Canadian Filmmakers Distribution Centre.

the outside door, moves his wife back in front of the painting, and begins savagely tearing at her clothes as she writhes in his arms. This outburst of physical violence prefigures the murder of his wife by his alter-ego Cluny at the close of the film, but it is also significant that this scene immediately follows Eulalie's experience of lightly touching the painting. It is an example, as well, of the powerful impact of such slow-moving or almost-still scenes in *The Far Shore*, moments that draw attention to material details, small gestures, and subtle shifts in the protagonists' points of view. As previously suggested, Wieland's cinematic vision identifies a productive tension between still and moving images, which can be linked to Guiliana Bruno's notion of 'emotive mobilization,' whereby the transition from stillness to movement is propelled by an affective momentum. Interestingly, in the final scene of the film, Ross himself is at the centre of a composition where the minimal transition from stillness to movement is of overwhelming significance. Cluny has just exited the frame with gun in hand, talking of the abundant deer in the region, leaving the disconsolate Ross by the side of the lake (fig. 3.2). The camera frames the slumped-over figure of Ross, facing a markedly peaceful (and at last an unapologetically picturesque) landscape picture. Without advance notice, without a sound, and with minimal paddling, Tom and Eulalie glide slowly by in their canoe. Ross lifts his head as he notices the subtle movement, and he shifts position slightly, but he is transfixed by this apparition and apparently resigned to letting the lovers disappear into the landscape. It is when they have almost entirely crossed the screen from right to left that a shot rings out and the body of Tom is thrown forward in the canoe. Only at that moment does Ross leap up, shouting his wife's name.

Masculine Behaviour

The Far Shore puts on display a collection of male types, and it is against

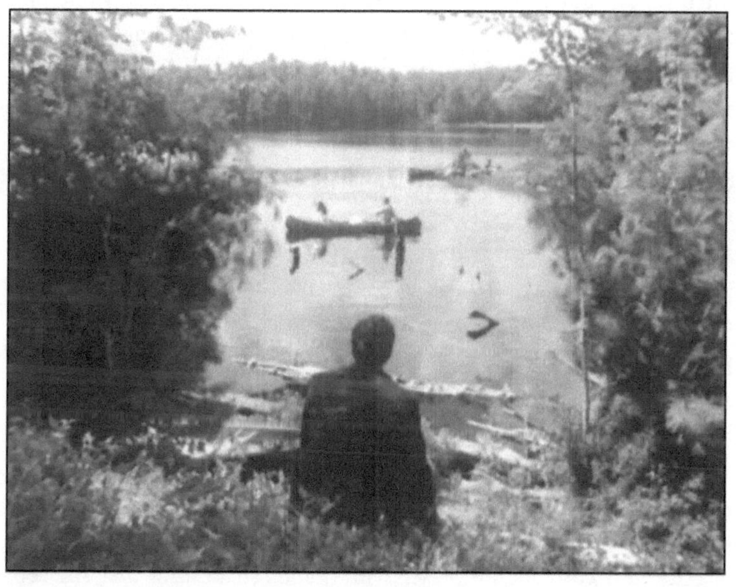

3.2. Ross watches the lovers' canoe drift by. Canadian Filmmakers Distribution Centre.

this masculine 'ground' that the figure of Eulalie gradually achieves coherence. Certainly, the film reveals that the social worlds and architectural spaces Eulalie moves through are dominated by men. At the start of the film Eulalie's brother and ex-fiancé are talked about, and even if the brother, Paul, is only briefly seen in a non-speaking role, while the ex-fiancé never appears on-screen, these characters are still important to the narrative, establishing the patriarchal parameters of Eulalie's immediate circumstances. Ross remarks about Eulalie's ex-fiancé, 'they say he'll be prime minister one day,' and so it is understood that her destiny might have been closely linked to the most powerful male figure in Canadian politics. Ross is apparently fascinated by this man and seems to imagine himself in some kind of competition with him that is both political and personal; when Eulalie has taken to her bed in a depression, he can only guess that she is still as enthralled by this alpha-man as he is. Eulalie's brother Paul, a lawyer, is evidently a wealthy and powerful man in his own right, judging by the palatial home he inhabits, but he is not an honest man; Eulalie tells Ross that he is being cheated by her brother and that, indeed, 'he cheats everybody.' When Ross is proposing marriage to Eulalie in the opening scenes of the film, he mentions visiting her in her home, but she quickly and with a tone of bitterness corrects him, saying '*his* home,' suggesting that she too has been cheated by her brother in some sense. The implication is that she hopes to acquire her own home by marrying Ross, although it is clear from the moment of the newlyweds' arrival in Toronto that Ross regards his house, its contents, and his wife as his personal property.

Ross is rich and successful and, although Tom tells him, apropos his determination to mine for silver, that he is already rich enough, he is apparently desperate for more money and power. His first on-screen appearances suggest that he has an amiable side as well, but gradually his character is revealed to be disturbingly similar to that of his best friend, business colleague, and former war buddy Cluny. Cluny plays an important role in this pageant of male types, because he is an example of what can only be described as toxic masculinity. Cluny freely expresses his sexual sleaziness, a propensity for violence, contempt for women, and an ignorance of art and culture. Behind Ross's veneer of good looks and civilized lifestyle lurks Cluny's brutish aggressiion. Ross might appear to play the dominant role in this relationship, but Cluny represents Ross's dark side, and this gradually comes to the fore in the narrative. Cluny starts the fight in Tom's shack, but Ross will end up throwing punches, too; Cluny makes crude advances to Eulalie when they are together in a boat, but at that point we have already seen that behind closed doors Ross is capable of sexual violence. If Cluny's opinions about art are laughably ignorant, Ross's appreciation for Tom's painting will be revealed as hollow, as once an art dealer informs him of its low market value, he withdraws his support of the artist, and from that point on will be interested only in Tom's ability to help him find deposits of silver on his land. Ultimately, Cluny might pull the trigger of the gun that kills Tom and Eulalie, but Ross is complicit in the murder of his wife and her lover.

Eulalie moves through this world of greedy and dishonest men, and Wieland's narrative makes us see them from her perspective. In cinematic terms this critical observation of male posturing and social positioning is already a significant feminist gesture. Eventually, when Eulalie realizes that she can make a choice, it is not simply a matter of one lover or another. Ultimately, this choice goes beyond her own life story, because the group of men who have dominated her life cover a range of superstructural positions: government, law, science, commerce, and the military.

In historical terms, the First World War can be regarded as a crucible of twentieth-century masculine identity. In the film, Tom Thomson's death – which actually occurred during the war– is shifted to its immediate aftermath, at which point it was theoretically possible to reflect on the carnage and destruction and to assess what victory had wrought. Scott Watson has written about the Group of Seven's project to paint the wilderness as paradoxically connected to the experience of the war. For the most part, no human figures appear in the paintings, but Watson argues that the spectre of (dead) male bodies haunts these lonely sites, so that 'the autumn flames of Algonquin's woods are the funeral pyres of heroes, the red maple leaf an emblem of a slain soldier's brave heart.'[10] The idea that images of nature (in its 'pure' Canadian incarnation) could enable a psychic restoration for a war-damaged generation was voiced by Lawren Harris. He spoke of his ambition to produce a 'more creative and magnificent communion than a communion of war.'[11]

The war is an understated but nonetheless key part of the narrative logic of *The Far Shore*. Ross announces in the speech he delivers to his employees that they are operating in a post-war economy, and at the first introduction to Cluny we learn that he was Ross's commanding officer in the war; Ross says, 'I followed him through hell.' It is difficult to imagine that any absolution for this 'hell' is available to these two ex-combatants, however, whether through art or nature. Cluny is a corrupt, morally compromised character, hardly the picture of a socially admired military leader and veteran. By the time the film shows us the two men in uniform, solemnly commemorating the war and its fallen heroes, we understand that the values espoused by Ross and Cluny will not help to make sense of the war, if it was supposed to be a defence of Canadian honour. In contrast to these military figures, *The Far Shore* briefly introduces another war veteran, an artist friend of Tom and a fellow sign painter, who is missing one arm. He might well be the 'old soldier' who told Tom what the Western Front looked like. Tom (along with some of his friends, we assume) represents a different breed of man – different in terms of character because he is honest rather than hypocritical, gentle rather than violent – but it is also made very clear that Ross & Co. occupy influential and authoritative roles in the public domain, and that Tom, as an artist, pursues his goals on the margins of power. Again, this critical perspective on masculinity and gender (part of the politics embedded in Wieland's 'romantic script') is achieved because *The Far Shore* is constructed from the perspective of a woman character who is extremely sensitive to these power plays.

Mixing Genres

Because of its delineation of a stultifying social world and its emphasis on gender relations, *The Far Shore* is reminiscent of the Hollywood tradition of the family melodrama or so-called woman's picture. However, in keeping with recent theorizations by film scholars, it is also possible to consider melodrama as a kind of sensibility or 'expressive code' that permeates a great many genres and types of cinematic production.[12] There is often a strong melodramatic component to films that are classified as thrillers or westerns, for instance. Another genre that is particularly dependent on melodrama for its effect is the artist's biography or 'bio-pic.' In a book about this film genre, John Walker discusses frequently recurring tropes about thwarted genius and points to how such films inevitably end up fixated on psycho-biographical dramas rather than on the artist's work; the conventional bio-pic recognizes 'works of art, therefore, only in so far as they relate to the life or express the hero's feelings.'[13] Here, the most telling cinematic paradigm is probably the blockbuster account of Vincent Van Gogh in *Lust for Life* (1956), starring Kirk Douglas. As Walker suggests, 'Douglas, by speaking all through the movie as if he about to break down or weep, conveys an impression of suppressed, violent emotion.'[14] In *The Far Shore* the art made by the fictionalized Thomson character is not so obviously the result of a tormented psyche. Mainly, though, *The Far Shore* does not conform to the conventional bio-pic because it is only obliquely focused on the character and accomplishments of the artist; Wieland's film complicates this genre by making the artist the object of someone else's desire.

There is only one moment in Wieland's film when we get a sense of the artist being overcome with emotion: it occurs immediately following the scene of Tom calmly concentrated on painting a landscape picture from his rocky perch overlooking a lake. It is from this position that he first hears and then sees Eulalie and Cluny coming towards him in a boat; then Tom puts down his painting materials and scrambles to a position of greater visibility. In the boat Cluny is rowing, chugging alcohol from a flask, and talking raunchily to Eulalie, his back to Tom. The lovers notice each other and their gazes connect across the expanse of water; the camera moves from one face to the other. At this moment the film provides a rare close-up of Tom's face, which has lost its usual composure and now unmistakeably expresses pain and longing (fig. 3.3). There is something rather startling about this moment when the audience is permitted to look into the eyes of the fictional Thomson, as he looks so passionately at the world, at the landscape, and at his beloved. Up to this point the film has tracked the melodramatically pent-up desire that emanates from Eulalie, but now the sentiment is visibly reciprocated, and their mutually desiring gazes expand to fill the cinematic space. At this moment, which is surely one of those breakthrough points in a melodramatic narrative as described by Brooks, the lovers' emotional life is no longer contained, and indeed it is so powerful that it suffuses and saturates the entire landscape. It must be noted, too, that this is a distinctly cinematic effect. The camera moves from one subjective point-of-view shot to another, while also providing the 'objective,' elevated position that situates both characters within the space. The close-up shots that are integral to this scene are non-naturalistic, however, because, while the lovers see each other across a wide expanse of water, they would not really be able to see what the camera reveals to us, the audience – the extreme close-up view of faces revealing that emotional upheaval. Thus.

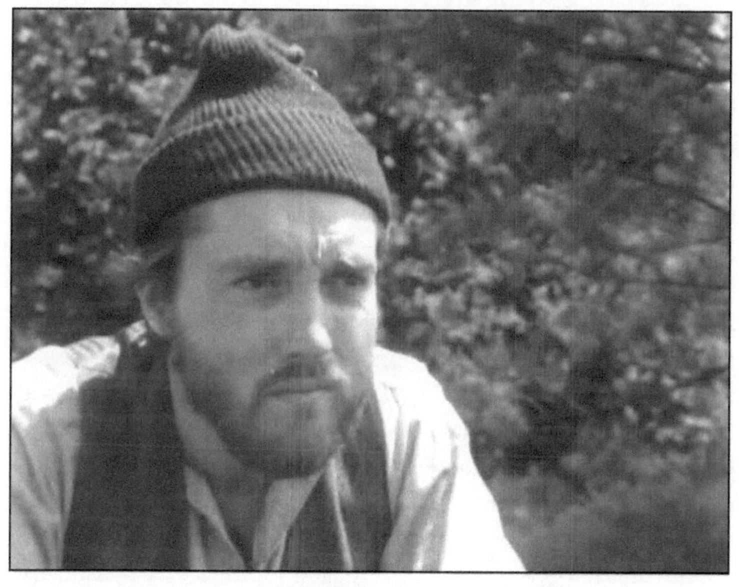

3.3. Tom's close-up. Canadian Filmmakers Distribution Centre.

Wieland deploys the sentimental excess characteristic of melodrama, initially associated with the Eulalie character within a specifically domestic and interiorized context, but then transported, in a manner of speaking, to the 'north country.' This melodramatic surge constitutes the film's basic narrative structure, and it is thus that our collective vision of the Canadian landscape is transformed.

The film's dual emphasis on heightened emotion and the representation of the land might also recall the Western genre, if Canada had such a tradition. Yet there are some melodramatically intense films that take place against and in relation to issues of land ownership and stewardship. Two films contemporaneous with Wieland's *The Far Shore* are worth mentioning in this respect. *The Apprenticeship of Duddy Kravitz* (1975), directed by Ted Kotcheff, tells the story of a character who is obsessed with obtaining a wilderness property in the Laurentian Mountains north of Montreal, for the purposes of commercial development – and the film makes it evident that Duddy's attitude to this piece of land is in keeping with his exploitative attitude to the people around him. Claude Jutra's *Mon Oncle Antoine* (1971) is set in an asbestos-mining region in Quebec, apparently some time before the momentous miners' strike in 1949 (around the towns of Asbestos and Thetford Mines), an event that is regarded as one of the triggers for the radical social transformation known as Quebec's *révolution tranquille*. Both of these films are set in the past (the 1930s or 1940s), which also is something they share with *The Far Shore*. Indeed, all three films depict past struggles over land, property, and identity, in a way that might resonate in the present day, even though Wieland's foregrounding of gender makes her contribution unique in the 1970s.

Outside

Eulalie's dive into the lake is such a significant moment in the film because the gesture has romantic and emancipatory connotations, but also because this action seals the tragic fate of the protagonists. Directly following the episode of Tom and Eulalie's charged visual encounter across the water, Ross meets the returning boat and informs his wife that everyone is to return to the city with him. Realizing that her husband is about to wrench her away from this place, and that he and his crony are equally intent on causing harm to Tom, Eulalie picks up an axe, which she repeatedly smashes down on a canoe and throws paddles and oars into the water; when Ross approaches to stop her, she strikes her husband with a paddle, knocking him down. Cluny hovers, apparently afraid of Eulalie at this moment, and he steps in to help Ross to his feet only after she is gone. Having asserted herself in this violent physical manner, Eulalie turns away from them and dives off the end of the pier. The action happens very quickly, but a striking still image taken from the film shows the delicately arched body of Eulalie suspended between land and water. This shot of a fully clothed woman suddenly diving off a pier is aesthetically powerful, and the next few minutes are equally remarkable, as Eulalie is shown swimming, her face luminous against the dark water. She has left one world (one shore) behind, and is on her way to another place, but the protracted swimming scene is a quasi-ecstatic between-state, which is also a moment of immediate, sensual encounter with the natural world. And if the film's main characters do have a fable-like dimension, it might be said that Eulalie comes to resemble something of a water deity. Not only does she enter the water and seem at home there, to the point that she draws Tom into and under water for their love-making session, but we then see that her character is water-like in its constant movement and shape-shifting (and it is surely no coincidence that she continually plays Debussy's watery mood music). The dive and subsequent swim also indicate a rupture with the many episodes throughout the film where Eulalie is looking out at the landscape – wistfully, melancholically, passively: she stands gazing out at the river in the opening scene; she stares out the car window at the scenery whizzing by on her way to Toronto; she stops to look out the windows of Ross's house on more than one occasion. Eulalie's swim ends when she reaches Tom's canoe, which seems to be adrift as the artist lies stretched out sleeping.

In turning to Tom, Eulalie reaches out for something – some realm of pleasure and freedom that is seemingly available on the 'far shore.' Swimming towards Tom, she simultaneously registers her desire for the wildness and otherness of the natural environment, and here it is important that the figure of Tom Thomson is so closely identified with the land. In this respect I disagree with Sherrill Grace's suggestion that by the end of the film Eulalie has become synonymous with the nature that Thomson and his Group of Seven colleagues set out to conquer: 'Her only function, when she joins him on the far shore, is to be his *terra incognita*, his wilderness, his inspiration and muse.'[15] Instead, the reverse can be argued, that Tom becomes *her* wilderness, *her* inspiration, and that Wieland productively confuses the gender/nature question. Since the camera has so closely followed Eulalie throughout the entire film and made possible the viewer's identification with this character, we understand that her desire has been setting things in motion, which culminates in the dramatic dive and ensuing swim. This represents a new kind of figure/ground relationship, because here we have a female figure measuring herself, testing herself, against the otherness of nature. Nor is it a simple reversal, whereby Nature is now to be identified with the male gender. Instead, it is as if Eulalie and Tom get together at the very moment when the radical alterity of nature takes over. The 'far shore' is not nature that is tamed, known, or even attainable ... but it is a utopian glimpse that the natural world offers up to human history and human consciousness.

The mythic dimension of *The Far Shore* is primarily rendered possible because of the role played by landscape. I use the word *role* deliberately here to suggest that the natural environment becomes, by the end of the film, much more than a neutral or beautiful background, and instead achieves a kind of agency and narrative force in relation to the human characters. The vectors of desires and gazes in Wieland's film are complicated by the impact of the natural environment. And the erotic figuration of man/woman does not, in a sense, take place against or even in nature, but rather *with* nature.

Conclusion: Melodramatic Landscape

In dictionaries and overviews of Canadian film it is sometimes implied that *The Far Shore* was deemed a fiasco from the moment of its release in 1976,[1] but this perception is inaccurate. It really does seem that the circumstances of the film's reception have been forgotten or misunderstood: after a study of the accumulated critical responses to the film that appeared in journals and newspapers, it is nonetheless clear that Wieland's film was taken seriously at the time of its release, and that it garnered many thoughtful and appreciative reviews. When the American weekly entertainment trade newspaper *Variety* predicted that Wieland's film was likely to be a hit on the alternative, 'art house' circuit – 'The *Far Shore* is a good bet for art houses everywhere and, carefully handled, might go in general release' – this was hardly a minority opinion.[2] In Canada, Katherine Gilday, Barbara Halpern Martineau, Douglas Fetherling, and Peter Harcourt are some of the authors who wrote in-depth, probing reviews of the film. Such texts are part of a burst of strong critical writing about *The Far Shore*, which in itself constitutes an important episode in the history of Canadian cinema, and this intelligent criticism is an indication of how *The Far Shore* succeeded in triggering discussion and debate.

The point is that the film was neither ignored nor casually dismissed, and even the negative response is interesting for the sheer length of the articles produced and the sophistication of the arguments mounted against Wieland. Significantly, contemporaneous reviewers of *The Far Shore* addressed a range of political issues as they analysed and interpreted the film. It is important to remember Wieland's comment, that she was setting out to make a political film, embedded in a romance. So we find Gilday recognizing that Wieland's film offers a glimpse of what happens behind 'the gilded facades of this hypocritical WASP society.'[3] Martineau addresses ecological politics when she says that '*The Far Shore* is rooted in the reality of the Canadian landscape, in the reality of destruction of that landscape by willfully ignorant men.'[4] Insights about contemporary gender politics are apparent in many reviews. Fetherling discusses Wieland's feminist perspective, while remarking that the male characters are nonetheless complex, and that the Ross and Cluny characters 'are more representatives of their class and culture than symbols of their gender.'[5] Reviewers did indeed acknowledge that the (fictional) love story was shot through with (real) political questions related to nationhood, social class, ecology, and gender. Peter Harcourt finished his review with the comment that *The Far Shore* was 'a film which has political significance for the whole Canadian nation.'[6]

This is not to say that the critics were uniformly positive, as the melodramatic, tragic, slow-moving story was not to everyone's taste, nor was Wieland's anti-naturalistic delineation of the main characters, each of whom carries a heavy symbolic burden. Nonetheless, Judy Steed, who worked alongside Wieland over several years to fund-raise and produce *The Far Shore*, says that Wieland was by and large not disappointed with the critical response, although she was certainly very frustrated about the poor distribution accorded to her film.[7] *The Far Shore* would not become the box-office success predicted by *Variety*. However, by the time of the film's release Wieland was already conceiving of *The Far Shore* as her first effort in the universe of feature films, and if this initial effort was flawed in certain ways, she intended to forge ahead and make other films, building on what she had learnt and accomplished in its making. Steed and Wieland acquired the rights to Margaret Laurence's novel *The Diviners* as the next project the two women would develop together. It is fascinating to consider what Wieland might have done with Laurence's complex (and comparably melodramatic!) story, but unfortunately, her second feature film was never made. It does seem that the gruelling process of amassing funding and resources over several years took its toll on Wieland; instead of developing her new career as a maker of Canadian feature films, she turned to smaller-scale projects and by the 1980s had regained an interest in painting.

In a sense *The Far Shore* was destined to be a 'one-off' in the artist's career, even while it is entirely in keeping with her preoccupations and passions throughout the 1960s and 1970s. While her feature film does not share the style of the earlier experimental films, *The Far Shore* must nonetheless be regarded as an experiment – in its cross-pollination of cinematic and visual art genres. And if some film scholars have been reluctant to recognize the aesthetic worth of Wieland's project, from an art-historical point of view what Joyce Wieland did with the landscape genre is radical, original, and experimental in the most profound sense. By revisiting Canadian landscape painting (epitomized by the work of Tom Thomson) through the medium of film and through the narratological and affective drive of the movies, Wieland sets the still landscape in motion. (In the 1971 bookwork that announced *The Far Shore*, the phrase 'a movie by Joyce Wieland' appeared, and this colloquial term does indeed suggest a pop-cultural world of entertainment rather than the experimental-film community she had hitherto contributed to.) Throughout this process, landscape does not figure as mere image, as a still image, or as the product of one person's imagination. Instead, in accordance with the words of Alexander Wilson, *The Far Shore* implies that 'Landscape is a way of seeing the world, and imagining our relationship to nature. It is something we think, do, and make as a social collective.'[8]

By the end of the film, it must be noted, the landscape does almost stop moving and does apparently revert to an 'autonomous' image of nature as the story violently ends. After shots of Tom's body in the water and Eulalie's floating hat, the camera seems to casually wander away from the scene of the crime, lingering over the surface of the water, with its pattern of aquatic plants, its spectacle of flickering light and shadow. But this gorgeous landscape imagery can less than ever be appreciated on its own, as it has been thoroughly entwined with the film's narrative and is now associated with the death of the story's heroes. As Laura Mulvey has noted about the endings of films, 'Of all the means of achieving narrative stasis, death has a particular tautological appeal, a doubling of structure and content.'[9] In *The Far Shore* the content in question includes the natural environment. By providing her audience with these moments of pathos and stillness at the very end of the film, Wieland reinforces once more that landscape has been thoroughly integrated into the narrative structure of the film.

As Joyce Wieland is now recognized as one of the most important Canadian artists of the mid-twentieth century, this film deserves to be seen by a new generation of viewers precisely because the film is in many ways the culmination of an exploratory and innovative art practice. It is more specifically Wieland's approach to landscape that remains compelling from a contemporary point of view, as we continue to grapple with the problem of how to represent a destabilized natural world. Wieland's artworks and films show – in terms that are more timely than ever – that the artistic practice of making landscape images does not occur in an ecological vacuum.

If Joyce Wieland's landscape sensibility was, generally speaking, informed by her environmental activism, as mentioned in chapter 2, it was the James Bay hydroelectric project that became the ecological flashpoint of the day, while the script was under development and as the film assumed a coherent shape. Of course, the Canadian territory has always been used and adapted by its human inhabitants, but the James Bay Project represented a new level of imagining how 'the North' could be appropriated, transformed, and made profitable. The scale of the James Bay intervention was monumental: entire rivers were diverted, ecosystems destroyed, and animal populations displaced, while human settlements and memories disappeared under the flood waters. This most recent 'development' of northern lands showed how profoundly and irrevocably the natural environment could be altered. This was the new environmental battleground Wieland was trying to come to terms with as an artist in the 1970s, and, to some extent at least, it was a contemporary sense of ecological crisis that she projected onto the past, and into the landscape of Tom Thomson. *The Far Shore* does not treat Canadian history and Canadian art history as sacrosanct or immutable. Rather, Wieland's fictionalized past comes into focus as it enters (her) present-day consciousness. As Walter Benjamin wrote, 'To articulate the past historically does not mean to recognize it "the way it really was" ... It means to seize hold of a memory as it flashes up at a moment of danger.'[10] So Thomson, his landscape art, and his historical moment are resurrected by Wieland, and these flickering images have the potential to illuminate the present-day situation.

By the end of the film the protagonists have been murdered and the Canadian landscape is bloodstained. Blood seeps (melodramatically, of course) into the vision we have of Tom Thomson and into the vision of the land Thomson created for posterity. If many Canadians already feel vaguely sad about Tom Thomson's death, it is as if Wieland wants us to feel sad all over again and to grieve collectively, even though this time we'll mourn his death for different reasons. *The Far Shore* asks us – the viewers of the film – to bear witness as members of Canada's 'old-boy' elite pull the trigger and kill the beloved national hero. This sudden death is all the more unfortunate because Thomson/Tom had fallen in love, in a way that would surely have transformed his life and his art. Then, because the Tom character's destiny is linked to Eulalie, her death becomes part of the greater national tragedy: we also mourn the fact that this woman, who was only just breaking free, was on the verge of discovering the Canadian landscape on her own terms.

Because the lovers are murdered, they fail to achieve their goal, which can be described in coded form as 'the far shore.' But the film nonetheless provides a sense of how people go about trying to escape from social constraints, from morally corrupt individuals, from a rapacious attitude towards the land, and from the threat of violence. What is this place they are heading to? We understand something about where they are going because Wieland's story makes evident what they are fleeing from and what they have set themselves against. When Eulalie has joined Tom and they decide to run away (paddle away) together, he says simply, 'I know a place.' We have indeed been previously informed that Tom knows this terrain intimately. But the destination the lovers have in mind – the 'far shore' they are reaching for – is also an imagined landscape, a site of refuge; a place of ecological, aesthetic, and sexual bliss.

With *The Far Shore* Wieland inserts a set of figures into a landscape that was apparently 'empty,' 'pure,' and 'wild,' and with this gesture she reminds us that the landscape was never empty in the first place. *The Far Shore* also implies, though, that for a Canadian artist to aesthetically interpret the land, it is still necessary to find a way through the wilderness imagery created by Thomson and the Group of Seven. In recent years contemporary artists have continued to revisit, remix, and culturally recycle the art of the Group of Seven, as well as the life and death of Tom Thomson, bringing their own sense of politics or sentiment to the encounter with nature. While many examples could be brought forward, one of the most striking pictorial reinterpretations of Thomson's death scene is Peter Doig's painting *Canoe Lake* (1997).[11] Doig is now one of the most renowned painters in the international art world, and he has strong ties to Canada, having lived here as a child and again as a young adult. Many of the paintings he made during the 1980s and 1990s are landscapes that include references to distinctively Canadian modernist gestures and styles of painting. While Wieland overlaid a melodramatic, cinematic story on the art and figure of Tom Thomson, it can be said that Doig's painting of an eerily drifting canoe accomplishes something similar, except that here the scene of Thomson's death is filtered through an image taken from the shlock-horror movie *Friday the 13th*. The resulting landscape painting rivals anything by the Group of Seven in its play of coloured light, shadows, reflections, and atmospheric effects. Yet it is the hybridity of this image that allows Doig, like Wieland before him, to introduce contemporary ideas and technologies, narrative momentum, and a new sense of pathos into the Canadian landscape. In such ways the landscape comes back to life.

Production Credits

Director

Joyce Wieland

Writers

Bryan Barney
Joyce Wieland

Cast

Céline Lomez
Lawrence Benedict
Frank Moore
Sean McCann
Charlotte Blunt,
Susan Petrie,
Jean Carignan
Cosette Lee
Don LeGros
Leo Leyden
Murray Westgate
Aviva Gerson
David Bolt
Colette Sharp
Dianne Lawrence
Jill Galer
Janet Doherty
Rachel Barney
Keith Craig

Producers

Pierre Lamy
Judy Steed
Joyce Wieland

Music

Douglas Pringle

Director of Photography

Richard Leiterman

Film Editor

George Appleby
Brian French

Casting

Karen Hazzard

Production Design

Ann Pritchard

Set Design

Gerry Holmes

Wardrobe

Aleida McDonald

Makeup

Kathy Southern
Bill Morgan

Production Company

Far Shore Inc.

Consulting Director

André Théberge

Sound Editor

Marcel Pothier

Running time

105 minutes

Further Viewing

Artist on Fire: The Art of Joyce Wieland. Kay Armatage, 1987
Kamouraska. Claude Jutra, 1973
Invisible Adversaries. Valie Export, 1976
Rat Life and Diet in North America. Joyce Wieland, 1968
Reason Over Passion. Joyce Wieland, 1969

Notes

Introduction

1 Anne Wordsworth, 'An Interview with Joyce Wieland, *Descant* 8/9 (Spring/ Summer 1974): 108.

2 Emily Carr is another artist who has inspired cultic devotion, and it is interesting to note that Wieland considered the possibility, at least briefly, that the romance in her story would take place between Thomson and Carr.

3 Robert Stacey, 'The Myth – and Truth – of the True North,' in O'Brian and White, *Beyond Wilderness*, 259.

4 Marshall Delaney, 'Wielandism: A Personal Style in Full Bloom,' *Saturday Night*, May 1976, 77.

5 On Donald Sutherland's being offered the part of Tom, see Martin Knelman, 'Sutherland: From Hart House to Locust,' *Globe and Mail*, 17 May 1975, 32.

6 Landsberg, 'Joyce Wieland: Artist in Movieland,' *Chatelaine*, October 1976, 58.

7 Levinsohn, 'Skin Deep,' *Maclean's*, 18 October 1976, 78.

8 Martineau, '*The Far Shore*: A Film about Violence, A Peaceful Film about Violence,' *Cinema Canada*, April 1976, 22.

9 Ord, 'An Essay on Canadian (Film),' *Cinema Canada*,Summer 1977, 41.

10 Wieland's reliance on everyday domestic materials and subject matter is mocked and she is disparagingly referred to as 'Joyce the housewife' in

Tom Rossiter, 'Weiland [*sic*] vs. Picasso: Patriotism's Absurdities Lose to Art,' *Ottawa Citizen*, 7 August 1971, 72.

11 Rabinovitz, 'Interview with Joyce Wieland,' 10.

12 Leroux, Review of *The Far Shore*, *Séquences* 86 (1976): 41, 42.

13 Gilday, 'How Joyce Wieland's Ambitious Movie Wound up on Canoe Lake with Half a Paddle,' *Books in Canada* 6 (February 1977): 31.

14 Martineau, '*The Far Shore*,' 22.

15 Harcourt, 'Joyce Wieland's *The Far Shore*,' *Take One* 2 (May 1976): 65.

16 Gardner, 'The Far Shore,' *Variety*, 18 August 1976, 22.

17 Gilday, 'Joyce Wieland's Ambitious Movie' 31.

18 Regarding colour, it is interesting to compare the relatively restrained coloration of Wieland's film with the intense, saturated colours of the NFB production of 1944, which echo much more explicitly the splashes of red leaf and cerulean blue water to be found in the painted surfaces by Thomson and the Group.

19 Rabinovitz, 'The Far Shore,' 29.

20 Ibid., 30.

21 Armatage, 'Joyce Wieland,' 93.

22 Longfellow, 'Gender, Landscape, and Colonial Allegories,' 171.

23 Rabinovitz, 'Interview with Joyce Wieland,' 12.

24 Grace, *Inventing Tom Thomson*, 8.

25 Leslie Dawn reminds us that Thomson's apotheosis as the central figure of modern Canadian art was by no means a foregone conclusion. When Thomson and the Group of Seven were exhibited internationally in the 1920s, the French critics were unconvinced by the National Gallery's rhetoric and continued to regard James Wilson Morrice, rather than Thomson, as the most significant Canadian modernist. Dawn, *National Visions, National Blindness*, particularly chap. 3, 'Canadian Art in Paris.'

26 Harcourt, *Movies and Mythologies: Towards a National Cinema* (Toronto: CBC Publications, 1977; originally a CBC *Ideas* program, Autumn 1975), 133.

27 Judy Steed in conversation with the author, November 2008.

28 Higson, 'The Concept of National Cinema,' in *Film and Nationalism*, ed. Alan Williams (New Brunswick, NJ: Rutgers University Press, 2002), 54.

29 On Wieland's political allegiances, see Sloan, 'Joyce Wieland at the Border.'

1. Becoming Cinematic

1 *Chambers: John Chambers interviewed by Ross G. Woodman* (Toronto: Coach House Press, 1967), 15.
2 Steve Anker, 'Rupturing Boundaries – Radical Filmmakers of the Sixties,' in *White Cube/Black Box* (catalogue) (Vienna: Generali Foundation, 1996), 307.
3 In 1965 Warhol announced, 'I don't paint anymore, I just do movies now. I could do two things at the same time, but movies are more exciting. Painting was just a phase I went through.' Cited in Steven Watson, *Factory Made: Warhol and the Sixties* (New York: Pantheon Books, 2003), 243.
4 Fleming, 'Joyce Wieland,' in *Joyce Wieland*, 53.
5 Rabinovitz, 'Interview with Joyce Wieland,' 10.
6 Wieland was perhaps referencing the innovative, early twentieth-century comic- strip art of Windsor Mackay and others who introduced additional storylines in parallel strips.
7 For an account of Wieland's early work experiences and her first encounters with film, see the biography by Jane Lind, *Joyce Wieland: Artist on Fire* (Toronto: James Lorimer, 2001).
8 Rabinovitz, 'Interview with Joyce Wieland,' 8.
9 Years later Smith would describe his dissatisfaction with the loss of narrative wrought by modern art: 'Where is the story today? I can't be impressed by anything wherein the story aspect has just disappeared ... the story sense disappears the more you're sunken in modern art.' 'Historical Treasures,' in *In a Different Light:Visual Culture, Sexual Identity, Queer Practice*, ed. N. Blake et al. (San Francisco: City Lights Books, 1995), 288.
10 Sarris, 'Films in Focus,' *Village Voice*, 18 March 1971, 65.
11 Gidal, 'Theory and Definition of Structural/Materialist Film,' in *Structural Film Anthology*, 4, 2.
12 Sitney, 'Structural Film,' (first published 1969), in *Film Culture: An Anthology*, ed. P.A. Sitney (London: Secker & Warburg, 1971), 326, 327.
13 Testa, 'A Movement Through Landscape,' in Elder, *Films of Joyce Wieland*, 79.
14 Sitney, 'There is Only One Joyce' (first published 1970) in Elder, *Films of Joyce Wieland*, 46.
15 Sitney, 'Structural Film,' 337.
16 This quote is prominent in the *Canadian Film Encylopedia*'s entry for Mi-

chael Snow. www.filmreferencelibrary.ca/index.asp?navid=92&layid=82&csid2=64&csid=299.

17 I would like to thank Laura Mulvey for calling attention to the fact that Wieland's determination to move from short experimental films to narrative, feature films was shared by her as well as other key artists/theorists/filmmakers of the 1970s and 1980s. Peter Wollen would write, 'For me the problem is to find a way of working with narrative. There was a real polarization in Britain around the issue of narrative – there was a strong anti-narrative streak in the Co-op and in the political documentary movement and as well as that a lot of the theory imported from France was strongly anti-narrative.' Cited in Michael O'Pray, 'Introduction,' *The British Avant-Garde Film, 1926 to 1995*, ed. M. O'Pray (Arts Council of England and University of Luton Press, 1996), 16.

18 Gidal, 'Structural/Materialist Film,' 4

19 Wieland's *True Patriot Love* bookwork was included, for instance, in the important exhibition *Global Conceptualism: Points of Origin, 1950s–1980s* (New York: Queens Museum of Art, 1999).

20 Buchloh, 'Conceptual Art 1962–1969: From the Aesthetic of Administration to the Critique of Institutions,' *October* 75 (Winter 1990): 107.

21 Bruno, *Atlas of Emotion*, 334.

22 Some years later Michael Snow's artwork *Plus Tard* (1977) would further develop this kind of blurred and in-motion photography of iconic Group of Seven paintings.

23 Wieland, *True Patriot Love* (artist's bookwork) (Ottawa: National Gallery of Canada, 1971), 41.

24 Théberge, 'Joyce Wieland: Drawings and Sketches for The Far Shore,' National Gallery of Canada Memorandum, 5 January 1977, 1.

25 Tausig, 'The Far Shore Combines Film, Art,' *London Free Press*, 28 October 1978.

26 Anker, 'Rupturing Boundaries,' 307.

27 Guattari, *The Three Ecologies* (New Brunswick, NJ: Athlone, 2000).

2. Landscape and Narrative (Tom)

1 For Wieland's comments on how she conceived of the three films as a trilogy, see Adele Lister, 'Joyce Wieland,' *Criteria* 2, (February 1976), 15.

2 Wieland, quoted in Alison Reid, 'The Film,' in *Joyce Wieland: Drawings for the Far Shore* (Ottawa: National Gallery of Canada, 1978), 3.
3 Lefebvre, 'Introduction,' in *Landscape and Film*, xii.
4 'Between Setting and Landscape in the Cinema,' ibid., 29.
5 Mitchell, 'Gombrich and the Rise of Landscape,' in *The Consumption of Culture, 1600–1800: Image, Object, Text*, ed. Ann Bermingham and John Brewer (London and New York: Routledge, 1995),104.
6 As the scholarly literature on the landscape genre is vast, I can only point to a few texts that address the complexity of this art form. On the structure of landscape images and the development of modern subjectivity, see Joseph Leo Koerner, *Caspar David Friedrich and the Subject of Landscape* (London: Reaktion Books, 1990); on the early articulation of ecology in the landscape genre, see Greg Thomas, *Art and Ecology in Nineteenth-Century France: The Landscapes of Théodore Rousseau* (Princeton: Princeton University Press, 2000); on the ideological effects of landscape art, see the essays in *Landscape and Power*, ed. W.J.T. Mitchell (University of Chicago Press, 1994); on the intersection of landscape and gender, see the essays collected in *Gendering Landscape Art*, ed. Steven Adams and Anna Robins (Manchester: Manchester University Press, 2000).
7 Grace, *Inventing Tom Thomson*, 124.
8 On the institutionalization of the Group of Seven, see Anne Whitelaw, 'Whiffs of Balsam, Pine, and Spruce: Art Museums and the Production of a Canadian Aesthetic,' in *Capital Culture: A Reader on Modernist Legacies, State Institutions, and the Value(s) of Art*, ed. J. Berland and S. Hornstein (Montreal and Kingston: McGill- Queen's University Press, 2000), and Joyce Zemans, 'Establishing the Canon: Nationhood, Identity, and the National Gallery's First Reproduction Programme of Canadian Art,' *Journal of Canadian Art History* 16, 2 (1995). Both of these articles are excerpted in O'Brian and White, *Beyond Wilderness*, 2007.
9 My essay in *Beyond Wilderness* links the experimental landscape practices of Wieland and Snow, when they returned to Canada after almost a decade in New York. Sloan, 'Joyce Wieland and Michael Snow.'
10 Walton, 'The Group of Seven and Northern Development,' *RACAR* 17 (1990).
11 Frye, 'Conclusion to a Literary History of Canada,' reprinted in *The Bush*

Garden: Essays on the Canadian Imagination (Toronto: House of Anansi, 1971), 12.

12 MacGregor, *The Wacousta Syndrome: Explorations in the Canadian Landscape* (Toronto: University of Toronto Press, 1985), 13.

13 Housser, *A Canadian Art Movement: The Story of the Group of Seven* (Toronto, Macmillan, 1926. See comments about Thomson on pp. 116–18.

14 'As he watched Jackson paint, Thomson's admiration grew and by January 1914 the two had decided to share a studio in the new building ... Jackson helped to correct the obvious faults in Thomson's style.' Denis Reid, *A Concise History of Canadian Painting* (Oxford: Oxford University Press, 1973), 140–1.

15 Housser, *A Canadian Art Movement*, 15.

16 'There was a streak of the dandy in him too, and he affected flamboyant silk shirts.' Harold Town and David P. Silcox, *Tom Thomson: The Silence and the Storm* (Toronto: McLelland & Stewart, 1977), 54.

17 Housser, *A Canadian Art Movement*, 124.

18 Jackson, *Maclean's*, October 1958, n.p.

19 Walton, 'The Group of Seven,' 173.

20 O'Brian, 'Wild Art History,' in *Beyond Wilderness*, 37

21 Philip Awashish 1972, quoted in Harvey Feit, 'James Bay Crees' Life Projects and Politics: Histories of Place, Animal Partners and Enduring Relationships,' in *The Way of Development: Indigenous Peoples, Life Projects and Globalization*, ed. Mario Blaser, Harvey A. Feit, and Glenn McRae (Zed/IDRC 2004). www.idrc.ca/en/ev-64526-201-1-DO_TOPIC.html.

22 Lord, *The History of Painting in Canada: Toward a People's Art* (Toronto: NC Press, 1974), 115. When focusing more specifically on Thomson, Lord describes *The West Wind* as a work of art whose allegiance is ambiguous: 'this is clearly a national- bourgeois symbol for our nation ... This is not the symbol of the working people fighting for liberation, but of a class that identifies strongly with the land and hopes to hold on to what it has. As an image of heroic endurance, therefore, *The West Wind* reflects both the aspirations and the limitations of the national bourgeoisie itself' (128).

23 Mitchell, 'Rise of Landscape,' 110

24 Wieland, quoted in Reid, 'The Film,' 5.

3. Genre and Gender (Eulalie)

1 Gilday, *Films of Joyce Wieland*, 31.

2 Kristy Holmes-Moss comments about Wieland's close-up on Vallières's mouth: 'the emphasis on the overt corporeality of Vallières, his "realness," is ... a way of using the sensorial and political to highlight the commonalities of the groups Wieland (and Vallières) sees as marginalized by capitalism: women, French Canadians and the working classes.' 'Negotiating the Nation: "Expanding" the Work of Joyce Wieland,' *Canadian Journal of Film Studies* 15 (Fall 2006): 35.

3 Hector Charlesworth, 1921, cited in Walton, 'The Group of Seven,' 175.

4 Mulvey, 'Visual Pleasure and Narrative Cinema' (originally published 1975), in *The Feminism and Visual Culture Reader*, ed. Amelia Jones (London and New York: Routledge, 2003), 45.

5 Thomas Elsaesser, 'Tales of Sound and Fury: Observations on the Family Melodrama,' in *Home Is Where the Heart Is: Studies in Melodrama and the Woman's Film*, ed. Christine Gledhill (London: British Film Institute, 1987; originally published 1972).

6 Kaplan, *Women and Film*, 25.

7 Rabinovitz, 'The Far Shore,' 122.

8 Cook, 'Melodrama and the Women's Picture,' 74.

9 Brooks, 'Melodrama, Body, Revolution,' in *Melodrama: Stage, Picture, Screen*, ed. J. Bratton, J. Cook, and C. Gledhill (London: British Film Institute, 1994), 19.

10 Watson, 'Disfigured Nature,'105.

11 Harris, quoted in Joan Murray, *The Best of the Group of Seven* (Oshawa: Robert McLaughlin Gallery, 1984), 11.

12 This concept is proposed by Elsaesser, 'Tales of Sound and Fury,' 51.

13 Walker, *Art and Artists on Screen*, 46. This passage continues with a reflection on the exaggerated expressivity of such films: 'The idea that art might be a construction ... rather than an expression, or that it might be the consequence of a host of social factors, is alien to the ethos of Hollywood.'

14 Ibid., 44.

15 Grace, *Inventing Tom Thomson*, 132.

Conclusion: Melodramatic Landscape

1 See Peter Rist, *Guide to the Cinemas of Canada* (London: Greenwood Press, 2001), 71.
2 Gardner, 'The Far Shore,' 22.
3 Gilday, *Films of Joyce Wieland*, 30.
4 Martineau, '*The Far Shore*,' 23.
5 Fetherling, 41.
6 Harcourt, 'Joyce Wieland's *The Far Shore*,' 65.
7 Judy Steed in conversation with the author, November 2008.
8 Wilson, 'Art, Geography and Resistance,' *Massachusetts Review* (Spring-Summer 1990): 236.
9 Mulvey, *Death 24 × a Second: Stillness and the Moving Image* (London: Reaktion Books, 2006), 72.
10 Walter Benjamin, 'Theses on the Philosophy of History,' in *Illuminations* (New York: Schocken Books, 1969), 255.
11 Doig's *Canoe Lake* (1997; oil on canvas, 200 by 300 cm) is in the Saatchi Collection, London.

Selected Bibliography

Joyce Wieland / *The Far Shore*

Armatage, Kay. 'Joyce Wieland, Feminist Documentary, and the Body of the Work,' *Canadian Journal of Political and Social Theory* 13, 1–2 (1989).

Elder, Kathryn. *The Films of Joyce Wieland*. Toronto: Cinémathèque Ontario, 1999.

Joyce Wieland. Toronto: Key Porter Books & Art Gallery of Ontario, 1987. Longfellow, Brenda. 'Gender, Landscape, and Colonial Allegories in *The Far Shore*, *Loyalties*, and *Mouvements du désir*.' In *Gendering the Nation: Canadian Women's Cinema*, ed.K. Armatage et al. Toronto: University of Toronto Press, 1999.

Rabinovitz, Lauren. 'The Far Shore: Feminist Family Melodrama.' First published 1986. In Elder, *The Films of Joyce Wieland*.

– 'An Interview with Joyce Wieland,' *Afterimage* 8 (May 1981).

Sloan, Johanne. 'Joyce Wieland and Michael Snow: Conceptual Landscape Art.' In *Beyond Wilderness: The Group of Seven, Canadian Identity, and Contemporary Art*, ed. John O'Brian and Peter White. Montreal and Kingston: McGill-Queen's University Press, 2007.

– 'Joyce Wieland at the Border: Nationalism, the New Left, and the Question of Political Art in Canada, circa 1971.' *Journal of Canadian Art History* 26 (Fall 2005).

Landscape and Canadian Art

Dawn, Leslie. *National Visions, National Blindness: Canadian Art and Identities in the 1920s*. Vancouver: UBC Press, 2006.

Grace, Sherrill. *Inventing Tom Thomson*. Montreal and Kingston: McGill Queen's University Press, 2004.
O'Brian, John, and Peter White, eds. *Beyond Wilderness: The Group of Seven, Canadian Identity, and Contemporary Art*. Montreal and Kingston: McGill-Queen's University Press, 2007.
Watson, Scott. 'Disfigured Nature: The Origins of the Modern Canadian Landscape.' In *Eye of Nature*. Banff: Walter Phillips Gallery, 1991.

Cinema and Genre

Bratton, J., J. Cook, and C. Gledhill, eds. *Melodrama: Stage, Picture, Screen*, London: British Film Institute, 1994.
Bruno, Guiliana. *Atlas of Emotion: Journeys in Art, Architecture, and Film*. New York: Verso, 2002.
Cook, Pam. 'Melodrama and the Women's Picture.' First published 1983. In *Screening the Past: Memory and Nostalgia in Cinema*. New York and London: Routledge, 2005.
Gidal, Peter, ed. *Structural Film Anthology*. London: British Film Institute, 1976.
Kaplan, E. Ann. *Women and Film: Both Sides of the Camera*. New York: Methuen, 1983.
Lefebvre, Martin, ed. *Landscape and Film*. New York: Routledge, 2006.
Walker, John. *Art and Artists on Screen*. Manchester University Press, 1993.

CANADIAN CINEMA

Edited by Bart Beaty and Will Straw

1 Bart Beaty. *David Cronenberg's 'A History of Violence'*
2 André Loiselle. *Denys Arcand's 'Le Déclin de l'empire américain' and 'Les Invasions barbares'*
3 Tom McSorley. *Atom Egoyan's 'The Adjuster'*
4 Johanne Sloan. *Joyce Wieland's 'The Far Shore'*

www.ingramcontent.com/pod-product-compliance
Lightning Source LLC
LaVergne TN
LVHW090809070826
844660LV00022B/1130

* 9 7 8 1 4 4 2 6 1 0 6 0 6 *